The Secret Everyone Knew

Natasha Mason

Natasha Mason,
New York, New York

Cover Design: Okomota
Editing – Layout: The Self-Publishing Maven
Formatting: Istvan Szabo, Ifj.
ISBN 13: 978-0-692-97590-9
ISBN 10: 069297590X

Printed in the United States of America

DEDICATION

This book is dedicated to every women and child that has experienced any form of abuse in their life. This book is for the silent sufferers who are afraid to speak out and feel ashamed. This book is also for the people who have lost their lives to domestic violence. I am your voice, your courage. In this book, you shall see that you're not alone and you too will overcome.

CONTENTS

CHAPTER 1
THE BEGINNING

My name is Natasha. I was born in Hartford, Connecticut. My story begins around the age of five with Laura, my mother. Petite 4 feet 11 inches tall, slim with short hair and a light brown complexion; some people may even say she was high yellow. I'm the same complexion as my mom, but I have long thick hair. We have a complicated relationship, so much that, sometimes I call her Laura and other times mommy. As a child, my mother and I lived across the hall from my Aunt Sadie. She was the oldest of my mother's four sisters; dark skinned with short hair, thin build and about 5 feet tall. All her nieces and nephews called her Auntie, and to us, she was the mean Aunt. However, she was outgoing, liked clubs and parties. Everything was going well for the standards of a young girl, and I got just about everything I wanted because I was an only child. I liked going across the hall to Aunt Sadie's to play with my cousins. She had five children, three girls, and two boys. I was close to Irene, the second oldest of Aunt Sadie's children. Although she was my cousin, to me, she was like a sister. Irene was also outgoing and very verbal like her mother. We went to the same school, were the same age, and dressed alike at times. I liked being the only child. It was just Laura and I. Everywhere Laura went I was right there with her.

Although Auntie Sadie often partied, she was very strict not just with her children, but with all her nieces and nephews. Shortly after living across the hall from Auntie we moved to the apartment building behind where she lived.

When I was about six years old, Laura's friend Patty started coming over. Patty had a son named Lenny who was a year or two older than me, and I had a crush on him. We always played together when they came over to our house. One day, Patty called Laura and asked her to come over because there was someone she wanted her to meet. My mother went to her home, and that's when she met Jeff, a muscular, tall and dark-skinned man.

Laura liked him a lot despite the rumors people were telling her about him being abusive. I guess she didn't want to believe it because a few months later he was moving in with us. At first, things were good, then as time went on situations started happening. Jeff and my mother were arguing a little more than usual. Then one day, Jeff pushed Laura because of something she said. So, Laura slapped him. He grabbed Laura by the neck and shoved her against the wall and yelled, "Don't ever put your hands on me again." After that incident, I was going over to Aunt Sadie's and my grandmother's house more often.

One night I was in bed and felt someone in my room. I opened my eyes and saw Jeff standing in the doorway of my bedroom just staring at me. I didn't say anything. I don't know why I didn't call my mom or scream or something. He kept coming for a couple of days before I told Laura, she said, "The next time he comes to your room just call me, and I'll take care of it." So, the next night when Jeff came to my bedroom door I cried, "Mommy! Mommy!" Jeff turned around and began walking away from my room. I don't know what he told Laura, but she never came to my room. There was a part of me that was hurt because she didn't come to see if I was ok. The next day my mother didn't say anything about me calling her and I didn't ask why she didn't come to my room. So, I just stayed quiet and didn't say anything. I thought it was over but little did I know it was about to get worse.

About a week later, Jeff came back to my room but this time he came and sat on my bed and told me to be quiet. He then began lifting my nightgown up, pulled down my panties to rub my vagina. As I lay there confused, not knowing what he was doing was wrong, he told me, "You better not tell anybody" and then he left my room. I pulled up my panties, put the covers over my head and silently cried myself to sleep.

Jeff would always do Laura wrong, mainly when he was drunk. He would belittle her, hit her in front of people and wouldn't care who was around. Even now, when I see people that knew them both, they ask are they still together, one time someone said, "Jeff used to beat Laura so bad! I'm glad to hear she's no longer with him." Hearing statements like that had me thinking that if they knew why didn't they try to help her?

As I got older, Laura told me about things that happened in the past. One day, Aunt Sadie met Jeff and told Laura how good Jeff looked. She also told Laura that she may have to try him to see how he was in bed. Jeff and Aunt Sadie began sending notes to each other. I can't imagine what was going through my mother's mind because she was the one delivering the letters they were writing to each other. The saying love will make you do some crazy things, is correct. Laura stated Aunt Sadie kept telling her nothing happened, but I know my mother thought differently. Jeff continued coming in my room, and I continued to cry myself to sleep thinking Laura wouldn't believe me.

A couple of months later, we moved to Massachusetts where Jeff's family lived. He had three sisters and two brothers. We stayed with his mother, Ms. Hutchins and his youngest brother Farley. Later I found out we moved because we were evicted for not paying the rent for three months.

CHAPTER 2
THE SECRET IS OUT

Living in Massachusetts was ok, but I missed my family back in Connecticut. I would sit on the steps of Ms. Hutchins' porch and think about the times I spent the night at my grandmother's house with Aunt Priscilla, who was the youngest of Laura's five sisters. Priscilla was a petite woman, quiet and kept to herself most of the time. She was a dark complexion with shoulder-length hair. I enjoyed spending time with her. We would play school, store and this game called radio where we pretended to be disc jockeys. Priscilla was about seven years older than me. I started laughing to myself reflecting on the things we did together, so, I wrote her a letter telling her how much I missed her. I looked up to Aunt Priscilla, and I still do today.

Laura enrolled me in school, and Ms. Hutchins and Laura started working at a hotel doing housekeeping. Jeff would wait until everybody was out of the house, then he would tell me to come in Ms. Hutchins' bedroom (that's where I slept). As he began putting his hands in my panties and rubbing my vaginal area tears rolled down my cheeks, he would say stop crying.

On another night, he went a little further. I was around eight years old when he took some Vaseline rubbed it on my vaginal area and began to penetrate me with his penis. I started crying saying it hurt. He said ok but continued. When he stopped, he left the room. As I'm writing this, I ask myself why I didn't tell Aunt Priscilla or some other family member. I don't know if it was because of the shame I felt, the embarrassment, or what. I started going to church with one of Jeff's sisters; I enjoyed it. A lot of the songs I knew from hearing my grandmother sing around the house (she was a Pastor) with the organ and drums playing. It was great, especially when we would sing aloud. I loved to sing and didn't care how I sounded. Today, I know we were doing praise and worship.

At times my heart went out to Laura. Jeff would talk to other women right in front of her, and she wouldn't say anything. I don't know if she was afraid of what may happen if she said anything or where her mind was at that time. Her abuse would happen most when I spent the weekends at grandma's house. I wouldn't see the physical abuse until later, but people would say is your mother still with Jeff, and when I said yes, they would just shake their head. When she did speak to him about it, he would hit her, right where she stood in public or private. Maybe she just didn't want to let him go. (The Holy Spirit ministered to my heart as I wrote this section. A lot of women, including myself in past relationships sacrifice being mistreated in one way or another to feel the love from a man or to show him how much they love them).

One morning, I was in the bathroom getting ready for school and Laura comes in to help me. As she helped me get dressed, she asked if anybody had been touching me. I thought, thank you, Lord, it's finally going to be over. I answered yes and continued to tell her that Jeff been touching me. She said ok and that she was going to handle it, but later that day I heard Laura telling Ms. Hutchins about it and that she didn't know what to do. Ms. Hutchins said she would handle it when he got in. I was upstairs playing a board game when I heard yelling. Ms. Hutchins was asking Jeff if he had been touching me in a way that he should not. Jeff started screaming no and then pushed Ms. Hutchins down the stairs and left. I got scared. Part of me wished I didn't say anything because it appeared to make matters worse. The next thing I knew, Laura and I were at the Greyhound bus station going back to Connecticut.

We stayed at my grandma's house for a little while. I don't know what was said. I found out a couple of weeks later that Laura had started back talking with Jeff. Shortly after, they got an apartment together on Pleasant Street not that far from my grandma's house. I continued to stay with my grandmother and Laura would come and see me almost every day.

One day Laura told my grandmother that she and Jeff were going back to Massachusetts because Ms. Hutchins was sick in the hospital. We didn't know at that time my mother was pregnant with my sister Jane. Ms. Hutchins had cancer. Jeff and my mother continued going back and forth to Massachusetts. While they were doing that, I was having fun living with my grandmother who gave me everything I wanted. Everybody knew wherever grandma was going you would benefit from it. You may or may not get something from the department store, but for sure you were going to eat at a restaurant.

After a couple of months, Laura came and got me from my grandmother's house saying we were going to be in Massachusetts for a little while. We stayed at Ms. Hutchins' house, and my mother was still pregnant when she came and got me. She was close to her due date so I would go to church with one of Jeff's sisters. Laura told me when she visited Ms. Hutchins they had a good talk. One of the things Ms. Hutchins talked to her about was the many things going through her mind at that time. One thing was her regret of how she disciplined her children. She also told my mom "be careful of what you wish for because you just might get it." She continued to tell her how she had wished to die in the past and now things weren't looking good. The doctor was saying she didn't have long but she didn't want to die.

About a month had gone by, and Ms. Hutchins was getting worse. My mother had just given birth to my sister, Jane. I don't why, but the next thing I knew we were going back to Connecticut. I went back to grandma's house, and they were still living on Pleasant Street. After a couple of weeks, my mother found out that Ms. Hutchins wanted to see Jeff and my little sister. Laura told Jeff. He said ok and continued doing whatever he was doing. For three days, straight Ms. Hutchins asked for Jeff. After the 3rd day, Ms. Hutchins died. Laura told me one day that Jeff shared his regret of not going to see his mother because he didn't get to tell her that he loved her. I didn't say anything, I just listened. Laura would talk to me often even though I was a child. I guess because she had no friends that came to visit and family barely came over. Although, I did think to myself that if he loved her, he had a strange way of showing it. How can you throw your mother down some stairs for any reason? However, I wanted to ask my mother if she really believed everything he told her, such as him loving his mother or anyone. I said this to myself because I thought how someone that displays so much violence and abuse could have love or kindness for someone, but I didn't, I just kept quiet. Deep thoughts for a child, huh?

CHAPTER 3
SOME KIND OF FREEDOM

I am ten years old, living with my grandmother and having fun hanging out with my friends that lived on the same block. My Aunt Priscilla was in high school at the time and still had a quiet demeanor. I always saw her as a sister, not my aunt and my admiration for her hasn't changed until this very day.

One day I was sitting in the dining room of grandma's house along with another aunt, Octavia. She was pretty, light skinned and her eyes changed color with the seasons. She was a thin woman. People often said she had a chance to be a model but made some wrong decisions in her life.

Back to the story, the three of us were sitting in the dining room, and Aunt Octavia told my grandmother, "Laura said that she loves Jeff so much that she would let her children go hungry just to give him her last." Grandma said, "I don't know what's wrong with her," she continued, "I think she's jealous of Tasha, maybe that's why she hasn't left him yet." As I sat there and listened I thought to myself, why would my mother be jealous of me? I didn't believe that she would let my sister and I go hungry.

Not long after living at my grandmother's house, Laura got an apartment on Peterson Street, two blocks from us. When I heard about it, I began praying, "Lord let me stay here rather than go to my mother's house." I was having so much fun being with my close friend Latisha, who lived across the street. We hung outside together all the time. Both of our families were friends. Aunt Octavia started going over to Laura's house more than usual. I hadn't moved in yet. Years later Laura told me that one night Octavia hid in one of the closets of the house. I don't know why, but I assume it was because she was afraid of Jeff. My mother said when she saw Octavia, she told Laura not to tell Jeff that she was in there. Laura said ok, and after that day Aunt Octavia stopped going over so often.

One particular day I was on my way home (to grandma's house) from school, and I had to use the bathroom bad. I went to cross the street. As I waited, the car was going slow, and I thought that I could make it. As I stepped out to run across- Bam! The car hit me, my chin scraped the hood of the car, and my knee scraped the bumper. As I lay in the street, a woman from an apartment building came over asking if I was ok. I said, "Yeah, I'm fine." She told me not to get up and just then some guy came over to me. I guess it was her boyfriend. They picked me up, and as they carried me into their house, they asked where I lived. I gave them my grandmother's address which was down the street. Someone went to my grandmother's house to tell them while another person called 911. I felt embarrassed because when the car hit me, I peed on myself. It wasn't long before Aunt Octavia came. She said, "I'm going to your mother's house and tell her what happened." I said, "Ok." She left, and about 5 minutes later the ambulance arrived. As they were taking my blood pressure and other vitals, I saw my mother, Aunt Octavia and Jeff running down the street. I guess Jeff came to be nosy. Laura asked if I was ok. I replied, "Yeah." The police officer explained what happened, and she got in the ambulance with me. On our way to the hospital, I told her that I wet my clothes. She said not to worry about it. Later I found out that the guy who hit me was drunk.

When we got to the hospital, I was still embarrassed. I didn't want to see the doctor smelling like pee, even though the smell wasn't strong. The fact of me knowing I had wet my clothes was enough. I guess the doctor knew because after the examination he said, "Let me see if we can find you some pants to go home in." After I changed, the doctor came back and told us that I needed stitches just under my chin. After the nurses prepped me to get stitches, the doctor came along with another nurse. From the way it looked, I thought I was having a serious surgery. While the doctor was giving me the stitches, he began asking me questions about school and the incident. I guess it was to keep my mind off him sewing my chin up. When the doctor finished, Laura called my grandma and asked her to pick us up. While we were waiting, Laura asked me if I wanted to go to her house or back to grandmas. I wanted to say grandma because of Jeff, but I didn't want my mother feel it was because of her I didn't want to go. So, I said, "I'll go to your house."

My grandma came and got us, and we went to Laura's house. I guess Jeff was waiting for us because there he was outside. He carried me upstairs. I don't know why because nothing was wrong with my legs. When we got inside the apartment, there was a mattress on the living room floor and a small television sitting on a table. Jeff and Laura began talking about how more comfortable they would feel if I had a bed in my room. They then asked me if I wanted to stay there or go back to my grandma's and without hesitation, I said back to grandma's house. I said in my mind, "Thank you, God! You knew I didn't want to stay here." So, Laura called grandma and asked her to pick me up because I had changed my mind. After I got there, it seemed like everything went back to normal and no one spoke about the accident again. But little did I know things were about to get a whole lot worse in the next few months.

CHAPTER 4
BACK AT IT AGAIN

About three to four months later I had to move in with my mother because she wanted me to be with her. They put a bed in my room, and I brought all my toys and things from my grandmother's house. I had a small television, radio, and pretty much stayed in my room when I wasn't outside. It wasn't long before Jeff started coming back in my room once or twice a week or when he was drunk. I continued to lie there with tears rolling down my cheeks as he would have sex with me. "Shut up and stop crying" He would yell at me. I guess he felt buying me a lot of gifts around Christmas time would make up for what he was doing. If I could have given the gifts back to be free of him, I would've. I began to isolate myself most of the time.

One weekend my mother let me stay the night at my grandmother's house. That same week, my mom was released from the hospital after Jeff beat her. He was arrested, and the officer told her if she pressed charges against Jeff she would be notified when he was released. Well, she decided to press charges against Jeff, but she didn't know he would be out that next Friday night. The police never contacted her. Laura was coming home from work humming and walking along thinking everything was great. When she unlocked the door to her apartment she began saying to herself, "Why is it so dark in here? I thought I left the lights on." As she got to the top of the stairs- Bam! She was punched in the face by Jeff, as she fled running down the steps she could see that he had brass knuckles on his hands. (As I write this now I keep asking myself why did she stay? Did anyone talk to her about domestic violence?) Not long after that incident occurred, something else happened.

My Aunt Priscilla came over to our house. She didn't visit too often, but I remember it was a Saturday. I don't know what happened, but from what I overheard her tell my grandmother, Jeff tried to touch her inappropriately and Priscilla took off her wooden sandal, slapped him with it and came home. She told my grandmother and her father who lived on the 2nd floor of my grandmother's house. The police arrived and took my aunt's statement, and arrested Jeff. The incident happened on the weekend I stayed at grandma's house. I was supposed to go home that day, but grandma said because of what happened to stay another night. I agreed. I guess she knew my mother was going to try to bail him out of jail.

My mother called when I didn't come home and asked why I wasn't back yet. I told her grandma said to stay another night. She then stated, "Come home right now. You know you're in trouble when you get in right?" So, I left and went to my mother's house.

When it came time for Jeff to go to court, of course, my mother was right there with him. I don't know what the judge said exactly, but all I remember was my mother asking Aunt Priscilla if she could drop the charges against Jeff. She relayed his message of being sorry and that it wouldn't happen again. She dropped the charges against him.

Time had passed, and after a while, I became friends with a girl that lived in the apartment under us named Lisa. We met another girl, Sharia who lived next door with her grandmother. We all played together along with Sharia's cousin Sham. One day Lisa and I were at her house, and she started asking if she could do something to me. Without asking what it was, I said yes. "Lay down and close your eyes," she said. So, I did. The next thing I knew; I was feeling her hands going in my pants. I opened my eyes and asked, "What are you doing?" She replied that we were friends and because I said yeah, she continued. I then said I had to go and I left. The next day she didn't say anything about it, and neither did I. We just acted as if it never happened. From that day, I noticed she wouldn't hang around me very much. She started hanging around the more popular kids on the block.

One night, as I was coming home from the store, Lisa was outside on the front porch with the other kids. As I walked past someone said, "Lisa there's your friend" and they all laughed. I could hear her mumbling, "She's not my friend." That hurt me very deeply and as I kept walking tears started to roll down my cheeks. A couple of days later she was speaking to me as if she never said such a hurtful thing. As I write this now, I'm asking myself why I never said anything to her about what she did and how it made me feel. I was so used to going through the situation with Jeff I guess it was easier for me to brush it off and try to forget about it than to face it.

I spent the weekends over at my grandmother's house when Laura let me. When I was home, I stayed in my room and only came out to eat, use the bathroom and shower. A close friend lived across the street from my grandmother's house. Her name was Latasha, and we always hung out together on my grandmother's porch. Everybody that lived on our street, around our age, hung on the porch, especially on Fridays. When it became too loud or after a specific time, Aunt Priscilla's father would tell all the boys they had to leave.

My grandmother began having church services in her home. She was an ordained Pastor. She made me the Sunday school teacher for the Children's Ministry and looking back now I wonder if she saw a gift in me. I say this because I took that role seriously. I didn't think I'm only ten years old, how am I going to do this or what do I do? She gave me the Sunday school books, I took it and ran with it. My cousins still talk about it now when we're all together. I loved watching my grandmother when it came to preaching, teaching or even if she was just praying. I loved watching her travel from church to church speaking the gospel which inspired me to want to do missions. One Friday I was at her house for the weekend, and she had just come from work. As she was taking her shoes off and getting comfortable, I said, "Grandma I want to speak in different places like you do." She replied, "Are you sure? Because it's not easy! You know there are some things you've got to go through as you reach different spiritual levels." I started thinking that I go through enough now so what more would I have to go through. To me, the worse the abuse became, the closer I developed a relationship with the Lord. All I could do was talk to the Lord about how I felt and cry to Him when I felt hurt because of the situation.

CHAPTER 5
THE FIRST PHYSICAL ENCOUNTER

We moved from Peterson Street to Roxbury Street, and when I could, I would ride my bike back to Peterson Street. I'm not sure why, maybe it was because the kids on that street were my only friends besides the people at school and they lived on the same block as my grandmother. Perhaps it was because I was somewhat afraid of making new friends. Whatever the reason, it didn't last long. I stopped going over there after making a few acquaintances near my house. Their names were Sabrina and Latera, and they lived in the apartment above us. There was a boy named Christian who lived on the 1st floor, and a girl called Little Bug who lived in the next building over. We all played together outside in the back of our building. Just before we moved from Peterson Street, my mother gave birth to my sister Jane. Once we moved to Roxbury Street, we would go to the park a lot, and on Jane's birthday, have cookouts. I felt hurt because my mother only celebrated my birthday once I think when I was three or four years old. Laura made me an all pink cake. My next birthday party was when I turned 40 and held at my daughter's house. I had fun, and the next one was four years later when my job surprised me, and two of my coworkers took me out to dinner (a friendship that will never end).

The sexual abuse continued, especially once my mother became employed. While she was working, Jeff would make me stay home from school every Friday. He would wait until I finished getting dressed and when I would wake him up to lock the door, he would say, "You're not going to school today." I would then go lay down in my bed waiting for him to call my name. Once in the room with him, the orders were to lay down next to him. The first time this happened I was angry because I didn't like being alone with him and going to school was my way of escaping from being in his presence. He kept telling me, "You better not say anything to your mother." He then stated with a smile on his face, "You know I can stop you from breathing." I answered, "No you can't because I'll start to throw up." He said, "It won't come up if I'm choking you. You want to see?" I told him no. I never told my mother. Part of me felt like nothing would happen even if I did tell her. After missing so many Fridays from school, the associate principal got in contact with my grandmother leaving a message for my mom. She wanted to meet with her because of my attendance. My mom scheduled a meeting with her and the principal explained I had been missing a lot of Fridays.

When I came home from school she asked, "Tasha why have you been missing so many days from school and where were you?" I began telling her I was home, just then Jeff cut in saying, "No you weren't. I'm here all day, and you weren't here with me." I couldn't believe what I was hearing. I thought he was going to say something like, "She wasn't feeling well, so I told her to stay home," but none of that happened. It was like he didn't remember telling me to stay home. Laura continued yelling at me and then I went to bed. All I could think about while laying there was why was I getting in trouble for something that wasn't my fault. The next day we went to my school and met the associate principal who had specific dates written down of my absences. She continued to tell her that they all fell on Fridays. Again, my mom asked me where I was on those days. I replied, "At home. If I wasn't at school, then I was at home. I wasn't anywhere else." Laura looked at me then thanked the associate principal for letting her know and assured her it wouldn't happen again. I went to class and Laura went home. I was on pins and needles all day because I didn't know what to expect when I got back. When I did, I was expecting Jeff to yell at me some more, but that did not happen. He didn't say anything. I don't know if it was because he realized it was because of him all of this happened or what. I didn't complain, I just went to my room and stayed there.

As the days went on, the sexual abuse continued. Just about every night Jeff would come in my room doing the same routine and I would silently cry every time. One night he heard me and said, "Shut up and stop crying. I'm not hurting you!" In my mind, I would say, "How do you know if you're hurting me or not? It's my body, not yours!" When finished, he would go lay down with Laura as if nothing happened. Although I didn't tell Laura Jeff started back having sex with me, I felt she knew.

Jeff messed around with a lot of women and although my mother knew she never left. Sometimes I wondered what was going through her mind and what was taking her so long to leave. One night a girl named Trina came over, and she ended up staying a couple of nights. I think she was around 18 years old and Jeff knew her mother when he once dated her. I guess she had nowhere else to go for the night, so she slept in my room on a mattress on the floor. One night I heard Jeff coming toward my room, I started saying to myself what the heck is he doing coming in here while this girl is here? The tears began to roll down my cheeks until I realized that he was still in the room, but he wasn't near me. So, I acted as if I was asleep. The next thing I knew, I heard him whispering something to Trina. I couldn't make out their words, but by their noises, I knew he was having sex with her. I told myself better her than me and thanked God that it wasn't me. I don't know if Jeff got tired of her or if he just wanted to have sex with her, but a day or two later she left.

Latera and I were still friends, but I met another set of girls named Sabrina and Tammy who lived with Latera and her mom. Sabrina was around my age, and she and I became close friends, or so I thought. Tammy was older than Sabrina by a few years. Sabrina was always upstairs, and I often went up there to hang out with her. My mother started to tell me that "Everybody is not your friend. They may act like it, but when your back is against the wall, then you'll find out who your real friends are because they won't leave you high and dry." I just said ok, but I was thinking she didn't know what she was talking about because she didn't have any friends come over. But then I thought maybe they don't come over because Jeff will screw them. Anyway, I didn't listen to her and thought I could trust Sabrina.

I began telling Sabrina about this boy I liked, named Lester, and how I started talking to him. His father owned the local corner store where everybody went to buy their stuff. When I went to the store, Lester would sometimes stand outside near the door leading to his house, and I would go in the hallway with him to talk and kiss. I don't know if I did it because I liked the attention or because he was the 1st boy I liked. I think back now as I'm writing and ask myself what drew me to him. It got to the point that whatever he asked me to do I did to make him happy. Then it happened. He was my first (besides Laura's husband). I didn't think it would happen in the hall (yes, he was wearing a condom). I thought he was my boyfriend, but when I began seeing less and less of him, I acted like nothing happened, which wasn't hard. One thing I learned to do over time was wearing a mask outside of the home. No one suspected anything.

When I wasn't home, I acted as if I had a great life and everything was fine, but at home, reality hit. Don't get me wrong; there was some laughter in my house. We would play card games like Uno or video games. Laura stopped playing video games when Jeff started arguing because he was losing. Since then, I don't think she's picked up a video game control ever again.

I started confiding in Sabrina. Not long after this, I found out Laura was right about her. Laura and I were talking, and she told me my Aunt Brenda came to the door a couple of days before to talk to her. My aunt told my mother to go downstairs with her for a minute. Jeff wasn't home, so Laura went. When she got downstairs, Brenda told her, "If you want to catch Jeff with Tammy (Sabrina sister), go upstairs from your back porch. They're up there right now getting it on." Laura looked at me and said, "I knew he was having sex with her before she told me." I felt sorry for her because I knew she was hurt. I wanted to ask her why she stayed with him, tell her that she deserved better, but I just hugged her and said wow. A few of months later, Tammy came to Laura and told her she was pregnant. I knew she was crushed because she looked down for a little while but quickly got over it or tried to get it off her mind. We didn't speak about it again until I became an adult, then she told me she knew the baby was Jeff's.

One night, Laura told me to go to the store to get some margarine, so I went upstairs to see if Sabrina could go with me. We left, but on the way to the store, we started talking about Lester. "You know Lester been talking to his ex-girlfriend," Sabrina said. I told Sabrina we should look for him. He wasn't in his father's store, so we started walking around to look for him. (I know, I know I should've taken my butt home like I was supposed to, but I was hard headed). As we walked, we rain into two guys that I knew, Dwight and Michael. Dwight liked me and always tried to talk to me whenever he saw me. Michael was his close friend. They stopped talking to each other and began asking us where we were going. We replied, "Home." We stayed and talked for a little bit before Sabrina said, "Let's go girl before your mother comes down here with a broom to whip you." We began to laugh, and all started walking towards my house. We stopped at the corner away from my house and stood in front of the church talking and joking around. Dwight turned to me and said, "Don't worry! If your mother comes down here you can hide in Michael's basement," We all started laughing. "Are you going to the house party at Michael's house?" asked Dwight. I responded that I wasn't sure. Just then we saw Laura walking towards us with my little sister. We all scattered, ran and hid in different directions, and I felt so embarrassed.

She decided not to chase me and turned around and started back to the house as she stated, "Tasha I'm not chasing after you." All I kept saying to myself was, "Lord, please don't let Jeff come down here." We went back in front of the church and continued to talk (tell me why didn't I carry my behind home). About five minutes later Jeff's car came driving down the street, and my mother got out of the car. I had no choice but to get in the car, dreading what was going to happen to me when I got home. When I got home, Jeff went back out, and my mother had this plastic rope she used when she exercised, and she began whipping my butt. She told Jeff what happened when he came in. He waited until about one or two in the morning to come to my room and started slapping me around (this was when the physical abuse began, I was 11 years old). Then he asked me what we were talking about while standing in front of the church. Before I could answer, he slapped me again. Then he took a rope that I used to play Double Dutch with and began choking me around my neck. I must have blacked out for a moment because the next thing I knew, I was on the floor and blood was oozing from my lip. He was taking the rope from around my neck.

He started asking me what the boys were talking to me about and I told him we were just talking about a party. He looked at me and said, "Don't let it happen again." I just laid in my bed as tears rolled down my cheeks. I thought "Why me?" The next day Latera came downstairs and told Laura that her mother wanted me to go to the store with her because Sabrina wasn't there to go and she couldn't go alone. So, my mother told me to go and come back. As we were walking, we saw Christina (Lester's ex-girlfriend) and her friends. "I heard you were looking for Lester last night," said Christina. Latera then cut in and said, "Yeah, but they didn't find him. They saw Dwight and Michael, and then her mother came, took her home and whipped her butt because we heard." I just said, "Whatever, we're supposed to be going to the store." Then Christina replied, "Oh Dwight already has a girlfriend." I explained I wasn't trying to get with him, but she went on to say, "Well, you can have Lester. He's not all that anyway." I just walked off. I felt so embarrassed about what Latera had said happened. I was so upset that I stayed quiet on our way back home.

A couple of months later I woke up to find the beginning of my period. I called my mother, and she said that I was a young lady now. I was dumb to the fact that I could easily get pregnant. And a couple of months later, I was. I told Laura, and we went to the clinic. I wanted to get an abortion because I felt I was too young for a baby. I was only 12 years old and especially did not want a child by Laura's boyfriend-husband. After I had the abortion, my mother said, "I was so hurt when you decided to have the abortion." What kept going through my mind was how she could say that knowing that Jeff was the father. Later she told me she didn't believe in abortions even if raped or molested.

Some months had gone by; I began junior high school and liked it. No one knew what was going on at home. I learned how to put on the mask, so to speak, while I was in public. We studied law in one of my classes and even took a field trip to the courthouse. I was so excited! I don't know why, but since then I'm so

31

intrigued with studying criminal law. Around this time, Jeff started committing burglaries.

One day there was a knock on the door by the police. Laura opened the door, and it was an officer in plain clothes (later I found out he was a detective), telling my mother he had a warrant for her arrest for bounced checks. However, instead of arresting her, they began searching through boxes we had in the house. Laura stated, "You can't search my home without a search warrant!" The detective answered, "This warrant permits me to do whatever I want," (from that day on I disliked Hartford police). The detective then asked, "Is there anyone to come get your daughter?" She said yeah and called my Aunt Sadie who got there just as they were putting the handcuffs on her and I cried as I watched them do it. My Aunt calmed me down and said to get some of my things so I could stay at her house. While I was getting me and my sister's clothes together, I remembered from class that an officer cannot search your home without a search warrant or your consent. I looked out of the window, and they were putting my mother in an unmarked car. As I was wiping the tears from my face, I was a little relieved only because I wasn't going to be around Jeff, but part of me was sad because my mother wasn't there. I loved Laura dearly despite the abuse that she allowed to happen.

Later in life, I found out that the detective drove Laura around asking her where Jeff was before bringing her to the station to be processed. They told her if she shared where he was she could go, but she didn't trust them. She kept saying she didn't know, so they took her for booking. I heard a couple of hours later Jeff was arrested when found hanging outside with one of his cousins.

CHAPTER 6
BEING WITH FAMILY FOR A SEASON

I stayed with Aunt Sadie for a while. During the time Laura was in jail, I only saw her once. I had fun at Aunt Sadie's house, but every time I went outside I took my little sister Jane with me. Until one day, Auntie said, "Go ahead outside and leave Jane here so she can play with the younger kids. She doesn't need to be with you all the time." When my aunt said that to me, I felt bad, and part of me didn't want to go outside because my sister looked sad as she walked toward the living room. I think one of the reasons I had fun was because I was around my cousins that were close to my age and we all got along. However, as I said before, Cousin Irene and I were super tight and continued to do everything together.

One day I was looking at some pictures she had in her room. I asked, "Who's this cute guy?" "Oh, that's just one of my friends. Do you want to talk to him?" she replied. She then began telling me his name was Mike. I suggested we call him. So, she did and told him she wanted him to meet somebody. He must have asked who because then she explained I was her cousin; I saw his picture and liked it. She told him my name was Tasha, and then she gave me the phone. We started asking each other questions (not realizing this would be a friendship to last for years to come). He told me he got some girl pregnant, but they were no longer together. I thought he was playing at first because he was nearly 13 years old at the time. We continued to talk about what we liked to do when with our free time and which schools we attended. We spoke just about every day, but then the phone calls became less and less because he wanted to come over. I knew my Aunt was not having that.

The more my cousin Irene and I hung out in the parking lot of the building where my aunt lived, the more friends I made. One person liked me, and I liked him. His name was Norris. He was at least six feet tall, light skinned and his hair was short. He was 16 years old, and I was only 13. At first, he was quiet, didn't talk to me and just talked to my cousins. He would act shy around me, so it took a while before we had a conversation. Later I found out he had an ex-girlfriend named Robin who was trying to get back with him. After talking to him about it, he told me that he didn't want to be with her and it wasn't long before we started talking. I don't know why I always fell for the tall guys with muscles. A couple of months later my mother came out of jail, and the three of us (Laura, Jane, and I) stayed at my grandmother's house. Laura was a couple of months pregnant before she went to jail and she was just about due when she got out. I was so happy Laura was with me again. That Sunday my grandmother was still having church in her house, and after the children

35

recited what they learned, I sang a song for my mom called, "I Miss You." She liked it, and everything felt good. Jeff was still in jail, and of course, my Laura started visiting him. I didn't like it because I was forced to go with her. I wanted to say, "He's not my man. Why do I have to go?" but I dared not open my mouth to say that.

A couple of months later, Laura gave birth to my 2nd sister Judith. I guess she liked J's for some reason. I had fun staying at my grandmother's house. I would hang out on the front porch with my friends until late and like always Aunt Priscilla's father would come downstairs and tell everyone they had to go home. That's how Norris and I stopped talking because every time he came over, my Aunt's father would say he had to leave. One rainy day there was a knock on the back door. I went to open it, and it was Sabrina from Roxbury Street, along with some other people standing in the driveway waiting for her. She began telling me she heard that I was talking about her. She then said, "What do you have to say now?" I replied, "If I have something to say I'll say it to your face. I'm not afraid of you." She then grabbed my hair, and I began punching her in the stomach. She let go of my hair and ran. Later I heard she told everyone that she beat me down and left me crying. At first, I wanted to find her and fight her again, but I couldn't find her. So, after a while, I just let it go because I knew what happened.

Jeff was released from jail, and we began staying at a hotel for a while because grandma wouldn't let Jeff stay at her house. I guess my mother felt she had to be where Jeff was because it wasn't before long before I started going to and from school from the hotel. Jeff would bring his friends over to drink and do whatever they wanted. I remember this one friend he brought over woke me up talking about he wanted me to meet somebody. I don't recall the guy's name, but he wanted me to go back to his room with him. Jeff kept telling him no. Later he said to me if I would have agreed, I would have been in his room with my legs up. I just sat there quietly wondering why he brought him there in the first place.

One day I was waiting for the bus to go back to the hotel from school, when I saw a friend of mine that I used to talk to named D or at least that's what we called him. "I haven't seen you in a while. Is everything alright?" asked D. I replied I'd been around and we would talk at another time because just then my bus came. As I proceeded to get on, he said he would be waiting. Part of me wanted to tell him what was going on in my household. At that point, I wanted to tell someone so it all could end. Then I started asking myself would it stop or would it get worse? It wasn't long before Jeff was back doing burglaries. My mother always tried to please Jeff, but he never appreciated it. Instead, he would put her down and belittle her in private and even when other people were around.

One weekend he started drinking and began hitting me. I didn't even know why. My mother was lying in bed next to mine; I'm thinking she was pretending to be sleep (I don't know if she was) anyway while he was slapping me he would say, "Shut up!" He then started telling me to take the pants off that I was wearing to sleep. He then took a piece of wire that he used as an antenna on his radio and called me in the bathroom. I was so scared I was shaking because I didn't know what to expect. When I got in the bathroom, he began whipping me with the wire. He kept hitting me until a little blood started running down my leg (I still have a scar on the front thigh area of my leg, today). He then told me to lay down in the bed, and he began to have sex with me. As the tears rolled down my face, I kept saying in my mind, "God, please make him stop." I kept repeating it until he stopped, then he went to sleep.

As usual, the next day he would act as nothing happened. About three weeks later I came home from school late, and he began asking me where I went after school. I told him nowhere, and he started hitting me. He was asking me why I was late. I just kept on saying that I didn't do anything. He continued punching and slapping me in my face. He then said, "Don't let it happen again." The next day I had a black eye, a swollen jaw, and a busted lip. When he saw my face, he just said, "You see what you made me do? I didn't mean to hit you that hard." I had stopped going to school for about a week. I don't know what my mother told the school, but no school officials got involved. Now scared or not I don't know why my mother didn't leave him or why she let the abuse continue with me. I never asked, but maybe I should have. Sometimes I think if I were more verbal things would have happened differently. However, I was never the type to voice how I felt until years after I left.

Not long after, Laura rented a car, and we all went to California. Before we left, Jeff had done some burglaries. Word got to him that they were going to have a warrant for his arrest on burglary charges; I guess he figured if he left before they caught him he wouldn't go to jail. We stopped at my grandmother's house, and she gave Laura a few dollars. Then we went to Bridgeport to see my grandfather, and he gave her some money as well. Then we were on the highway on our way to California. Around this time, I was 14 years old. No one knew that we were leaving. Even if she did say something, they wouldn't believe her. As we drove on the highway, all that was going through my mind was that I was leaving my friends and family and would be alone now. I began to change my whole attitude when we got to California. I didn't become friends with anyone, so there wasn't much joking around. I could act silly when I was around my friends because that was the only time I could forget about the abuse aside from when I was in school. Now don't get me wrong, the abuse didn't happen every day. For example, on the way to California, we were in Colorado driving down what seemed like a mountain. The road was icy, and we were going too fast. Jeff tried slowing down, but couldn't and hit a stop sign. Jeff got out of the car, saw there was no damage and continued to drive. In a way, it was funny. I guess you had to be there.

CHAPTER 7
LIFE IN CALI

When we got to California, my mind focused on what could happen next. We stayed at the Salvation Army shelter in Los Angeles, but Jeff couldn't stay with us because he and my mom were not legally married. So, he slept in the car. Every morning after we ate breakfast Jeff would be waiting for us outside in the car. We would go riding around to figure out where they could get money to stay at a hotel and then we would go back to the shelter. I started feeling sick every time we got in the car with Jeff, but once we get back to the shelter, I would feel fine. I went to the emergency room again, and that's when we found out that I was pregnant for the 2nd time. I didn't get much of a reaction from Laura, but Jeff wanted me to have the baby.

They applied for state assistance, and we left the shelter and stayed at a hotel in Los Angeles for a little while. Someone told Jeff and my mother about a shelter in San Pedro that was like an apartment. We could be there for a few months, so that's where we went. After getting into the shelter, my mother registered me for school. I had to go back to junior high school because, in San Pedro, high school began in 10th grade. Part of me was not up to going because I was 14 years old and pregnant although I wasn't showing yet. Inside I felt embarrassed and ashamed mostly because the father of my child was my mother's boyfriend-husband (they weren't legally married, but according to the state of California they were common law). It hurt that every time Laura made an appointment for an abortion Jeff always had an excuse for her not to take me. Now don't get me wrong, I love my son dearly and would do anything for him, but felt it was wrong to have a child with my mother's husband. I was wearing big jackets and shirts to school. It wasn't long before other girls at school were making assumptions that I was pregnant as I was trying to cover it up. When they asked me, I denied it. After about four to five months our time was up at the shelter. We applied for the Section 8 subsidy but were still on the waiting list. We went to Long Beach and stayed at a hotel.

I wasn't allowed to go anywhere. I'm assuming because Jeff thought that I was going to get an abortion. I was about six months pregnant before I began going anywhere with Laura. I guess the money ran out before the following month because next thing I knew we were leaving the hotel and staying with some lady that Jeff met. Me, Laura, Jane, Judith and Jeff stayed at this house with a woman we barely knew. I don't know where or how Jeff met her. I guess Laura just did whatever Jeff said because I never heard them argue about it. She had a beautiful house and an older daughter; I would say about her early 20s. We stayed there for a couple of weeks before we went back to the hotel. By this time, I had started going to the doctor and taking the prenatal vitamins and iron pills. As my baby was moving inside me, I just kept thinking how much I was going to love him. After I found out I was going to have a boy, the name Jack stood out to me, and that's what I named him. As time went on, I wished that I was working so that I could buy my baby some clothes; I didn't have anything for him.

A couple of months later Jeff was hanging out one night. I don't know what happened, but my mother told me in the morning that Jeff was arrested the night before. We went to the police station to find out what was going on and learned he was stopped by police who ran his name. His warrant from Connecticut came up, and Jeff was going to be extradited back home on burglary charges. I was happy because that meant we were going back to Connecticut. I continued going to my prenatal appointments. A couple of weeks before my due date my Aunt Priscilla came to California. She began asking me if Jeff was with the baby's father. I just said no and left it at that. Why didn't I tell her the truth? To this day, I can't answer that question because I don't know. Maybe it was because I felt ashamed and embarrassed because I was pregnant with Laura's boyfriend-husband child. Then it also could be because I didn't want Laura feeling bad or talked about by the family. I was having all these feelings but kept them to myself.

After Aunt Priscilla left, it was back to our routine of visiting Jeff and contacting places to help us with a ticket back to Connecticut. This particular day I went to the doctor's, and she began asking me if I was feeling any pain. I told her no. As she continued examining me, she explained, "Well you're having some good contractions." She began telling me she wanted to admit me into the hospital. I told my mom, and we took a cab because the hospital that accepted my insurance coverage was far away. On the way there I was kind of scared because my mother told me what happened to someone we both knew. When they were kids she said, this girl had a baby at 13 years old, and the pain was so severe that the woman had a stroke. I just kept thinking about that and praying to the Lord, please don't let that happen to me.

When we finally got to the hospital, they began hooking me up to different types of machines. The only thing I could eat was crushed ice, so that's what I ate while watching TV. The nurse came in and looked at a paper that was monitoring my contractions and she began asking whether I was feeling any pain. "No," I replied. She then asked if I was sure because I was having some strong contractions. In my mind, I just kept thanking God that I wasn't feeling anything. Not long after that, they moved me into a delivery room, and they told me to push. After a few minutes my son Jack was born, and I didn't feel a thing. My mother stayed at the hospital with me until I gave birth and then she had to leave the hospital to get my sisters because they were too young {one and three years old} to be by themselves.

Laura left them with the lady whose house we were staying. Because Jack was two weeks early, the nurse said he looked kind of small, and they wanted to keep him in the hospital for observation. I began crying and thinking they wanted to keep my baby. Laura called, and I told her what the nurse said. I don't know what she told them, but five minutes later the nurse was coming back telling me that I could take him home with me. I was so happy! All I kept saying on the ride back to the hotel room was, "This is my baby, and I'm going to pour all my love on him." At that specific moment, I didn't think I'm a teen mom with no job or how I was going to raise him, I just felt good giving love to my baby.

CHAPTER 8
WHAT AN EXPERIENCE

We were back at the hotel room, and my mom was going to agencies still trying to get help with our tickets back to Connecticut. One day while she was gone, the woman who we stayed with from Long Beach stopped by the hotel. I remembered my grandmother saying to me, "Don't let everybody hold your baby; especially if you don't know them." So, when she came, she told me Laura told her I had the baby and then she asked to see him. So, I held him up for her to see him. Then she sat on the bed and asked how long before Laura would be back. I told her that I didn't know and she left. When Laura came in, I told her the lady who we stayed with came by for a moment. I never knew her name. I guess my mother was fine with it; her response was ok. As long as we knew the person, it was ok. Although I did think she would've been upset with me for letting the lady in while she was gone, she wasn't.

The next day my sister Jane felt sick. Laura started noticing these marks on her hand. So, I went to the payphone and called my grandmother who was also a pastor.

To me, it all seemed kind of weird. Grandma told me to get some blessed oil and pray over Jane's hand, wipe it with the oil on a paper towel, then burn the paper towel. So, I got some olive oil from the store and prayed over it. Grandma taught me since I was little how to plead the blood of Jesus when scared or going through something. I also read my Bible often, so I knew some scriptures. If I didn't see it for myself, I wouldn't believe what happened next. We burned the paper towel, and it burned everywhere except where we wiped her hand. I went back and called my grandmother again and told her what happened. She then began to tell me to have Laura burn everything that the woman gave us and then anoint my sister and pray over her.

I told Laura what grandma said, and she began looking for something to put the clothes in to burn them. She couldn't find anything, so she put them in the tub, lit the clothes for a second, put out the fire and threw the clothes in the trash. I then put the oil in my hands, and as I began praying for my sister, she threw up what looked like chunks of pineapple. She hadn't eaten anything yet, and she definitely didn't have any pineapples the day before. After I finished praying and we cleaned up the vomit, I asked her how she felt. She said better and back to normal. I called my grandmother to tell her how everything went. She then told me to keep pleading the blood of Jesus over the baby and to be careful because that woman was dealing with witchcraft. I said yes ma'am, and she said that she would keep us in her prayers and we hung up. I don't know why Laura didn't call grandma herself to do what she told me to do and I never asked her. Maybe she felt she couldn't or perhaps her faith wasn't that strong at that time. I don't know why but I felt the need to act.

Every night, I would silently plead the blood of Jesus over everyone and ask God to protect us. Later Laura told me grandma said that woman was dealing with witchcraft and knew what to do. She said grandma used to deal with that a long time ago until one day she came back from New York and got rid of the candles and all kinds of stuff she had. She started going to church after a while, began studying to be a pastor and had been one ever since ordained. Even as I'm typing this now, I think about what went on that day. At the age of 14 years old I was praying for my family and me. Now I can't tell you what I said because I don't remember, but what I can tell you is when I prayed I didn't have to think about what to say. The words just came out of my mouth and the 1st time I had to pray in that manner. However, as you read later, it would not be the last.

A couple of days later my mother found an agency that paid for our tickets to go back to Connecticut, or so I thought. When we got on the bus, Laura told me we're going to Cape Cod, Massachusetts which is where Jeff's family lived. I was ok with it because I knew that we were going to go to Connecticut often for her to see Jeff. The bus ride to Massachusetts was ok. I was just excited to see my cousins, other family members, and friends.

CHAPTER 9
LOOKING FOR LOVE
IN THE WRONG PLACE

When we arrived in Massachusetts, Jeff's sister Reese picked us up from the bus station and we stayed with her for a while. One day, Jeff called on her phone and Reese told my mom that Jeff said he wanted us to go to Connecticut. Laura started saying that's not what he said the last time we spoke. So, we waited for Jeff to call Reese's house. When he did, he was upset with Laura for not going to Connecticut. I don't know what he told her, but she was upset and stressed out. She cried, and I just put my arms around her shoulders. As she sat on the sofa, I didn't know what to say. I just wanted her hurt to stop. Now some people may think why would I give Laura comfort when she knew what was going on and didn't protect me. My answer, I guess during those times I didn't think about me or why she never comforted me, I was happy when she was happy. I didn't think Jeff would touch any of my sisters because he was their biological father. He didn't see himself as a father figure to me, and I didn't see him as one either. I don't know what was said later, but he was alright with Laura being in Massachusetts, for the time being. We were receiving public assistance, and they paid for us to stay at a hotel.

I began high school, and at lunch I overheard a girl say that she had a child in the daycare of our school. I started thinking it would be good if I could bring my son (I had just turned 15 years old). When I got home, I talked to Laura about it, but she didn't like the idea. She told Jeff about it, and he wanted to talk to me on the phone. He told me not to do it and that if Laura were working, that would be different. I just told him ok but not long after that Laura permitted me to get a job. I was so excited especially when hired as a cashier, which was kind of my dream job because I liked counting money.

We were going to Connecticut on the weekends to see Jeff and would stay at my grandmother's house or a hotel. One weekend we stayed at a hotel, and I called Mike. I always stayed in touch with him as long as we had a phone. We were talking, and he asked if I wanted to see him. I told him where I was and what room number. Laura was getting ready to go and visit Jeff. I wasn't going to say anything at first, but I decided to tell her, and she was fine with it. I was so happy. Just then, Mike knocked on the door. At first, I told him to hold on a minute, and I closed the door, but Laura said to let him in. She and I took a moment to go into the bathroom to talk. My mother told me if anything happened I should go to Aunt Sadie's house. I don't know why she said that I thought she was just going to see Jeff and I never asked her what she meant. She then gave me $20.00 and left to go on her visit. I threw the money on the bed.

Mike then stated, "You put it down like you don't want that twenty dollars. I'll take it if you don't want it." I picked it up and put it in my pocket. Mike walked over to my son and asked if he was mine. I told him yes. Then we began telling each other how good we looked. Mike said, "Let's go to the bathroom for a minute." At first, I pretended not to know why. But then he said, "Let me show you..." All I kept seeing was how tall and muscular he was, not to mention his good looks. My son was asleep, and my sisters went with my mother, so I said ok and while in the bathroom we had sex. Neither one of us wanted or was ready for another child, so yes, we used a condom. Afterward, we talked for a few then he left. When my mother came back, she asked where I'd met him because he was cute. I began smiling and said Irene had introduced us a long time ago and we stayed in touch. Looking back, I don't know what my mother was thinking that night. I would have never let my 15-year-old daughter alone in a hotel room with a boy. I liked the fact that he gave me attention and affection I wasn't receiving from anyone else. To be held by someone I loved or thought I loved was terrific. After a while, we moved again from Massachusetts to Connecticut and stayed at my grandmother's house. I was glad because once again I was around my friends.

Some parents didn't want their child around me because I had a baby at a young age. Laura registered me to the local public high school. Everything was going well. I was a little upset when one day I was talking to

Mike and found out that I wasn't the only girl in his life. I called my cousin Irene and told her what happened. She was upset and said she was going to handle it. I began hanging out with the people on the street where my grandmother lived. They were mostly boys and a couple of girls that lived on the 3rd floor of my grandmother house. We would hang on my grandmas' porch until late night on Fridays and the weekends.

There was one boy in the neighborhood I started talking to named TJ. He was skinny, kind of tall and dark skinned. He didn't look all that good, but for some reason, I was drawn to him. We were on and off for about a year, only because I kept hearing that he was seeing another girl. One day there was a block party not far from my grandmother's house. I got permission to go, I saw a girl that I knew, and she told me she just saw TJ with another girl. When I asked where, she said, "Over by the basketball court." I went over there, made sure he saw me, and then walked away. After hanging out there for a little bit, I went back to my grandmother's house. The next time I saw TJ I told him not to call me anymore and that I didn't want to see him. I told him, "Go be with the girl you were hugged up with because you're not worth my time." He was trying to explain, but I wasn't trying to hear it.

A couple of months later, Irene called and wanted to know if I wanted to hang out with her and she had someone she wanted me to meet. Laura let me go and I left for Auntie Sadie's house only to see that Irene was still getting ready. After a few moments of waiting, Irene told her sister to tell Auntie that we were leaving. We went to one of Irene's friend's house, she called the guy she wanted me to meet, and he came over. His name was Henry; tall, dark brown complexion with muscles and all I kept thinking was Wow he looked good! As we started talking, Irene's mother called on their house phone asking her why we didn't tell her that we were leaving. I'm quite sure Auntie knew the address because she wasn't the type that would let her kids go somewhere that she couldn't get to if needed. She then told us the time she wanted us back. Henry and I exchanged phone numbers, and after a few minutes, we left to go back to Irene's house.

Now, she didn't tell me that she had told her mother we were going to be somewhere else until we walked in the door. Auntie Sadie met us at the door asking us where we went because she knew we weren't where Irene told her we were going. I let Irene do all the talking. Auntie Sadie was saying how Cousin Irene's best friend always called the house when they weren't together. She said, "I'm going to walk out of this room, and Y'all better get your story straight because if it isn't right, I'm whooping some asses." When she left the room, I told Irene to tell the truth of where we went, if not, I would. She came in a few minutes later and believed the story Irene told her. After that, we didn't hang out too much unless it was around the area where she lived.

Henry and I became close. We did have sex, and to me, he was my boyfriend although we didn't go out anywhere. As I write about this, maybe I was naive because when we were together all we did was have sex, at his house when his parents weren't home or at another property that his parents owned and no one lived. We did talk on the phone. At the same time, I had broken up with Carson, a boy I started talking to while Henry and I were on a break during that summer. I wanted a more serious relationship where we were exclusive such as his parents knew me and my family knew who he was. I know! I was too young thinking like that since I was 15 at the time. Henry didn't agree so we took a break then started back seeing each other when school began again. We dated for about three months then called it quits but continued to chat on the phone as friends.

Jeff was about to be released to half-way housing. I kept thinking why couldn't he stay in jail longer? He had served about a year. I know it was wrong to think, but I was happy. I didn't have to look over my shoulder all the time or be on pins and needles. We (my mother and I) started going to see Jeff. He then began to get weekend passes home and started spending those weeks at a hotel. Once, I wanted to talk to Henry so bad. I was missing him, and I couldn't wait until Sunday night to talk to him. So, when I was sent to get some burgers, I stopped at a payphone and called Henry. I didn't realize how long we talked, but when I looked up, I saw Jeff coming toward the pay phone. I told Henry I had to go. Jeff started yelling at me. When we got in the room, he started slapping me and asking me who I was calling. He said I should've asked to call my friend. My mother did nothing, and her face said, "Why did you do that?" When it was all said, and done, I had a bruise on my face, and I didn't go anywhere until it was gone. No one asked what happened; they just kept quiet about it.

We were still staying with my grandmother at the time, and I started feeling sick again. Every time I stretched out my leg, I would get a Charlie horse. I thought that I might be pregnant, but I wasn't sure. I took a pregnancy test and found out that I was pregnant. I knew it was Henry's baby, but I knew that he was going to college and I felt that he may not want to be in the baby's life like that. So, I did something that I know I really should not have done. I purposely had sex with Carson so that I could tell him that he was the father. Around this time there was talk about going back to California between Jeff and Laura. Before there was a final decision to go back, I told my grandmother what Jeff had been doing to me. She called the halfway house and spoke to someone there who asked me if it was true. I said yes. Jeff was sent back to jail, and my grandmother left because she had to preach in another state. I don't know if grandma was afraid of reporting Jeff to the police sooner or if she were worried Laura would go to jail too for not doing anything. I don't know the reason why she never said anything before that moment, but I was glad she did. My grandma was the only support I had. I just wanted the abuse to end, not just for me, but for Laura as well.

A detective came and took my statement, and then I spoke to another detective with my mother there. About a week later, Laura came to me and said, "You need to drop the charges. Jeff is saying they're calling him names." When I didn't respond, she said, "You're no angel either. I have your phone book with those boys' numbers, and if you don't drop the charges, I'm going to give it to his attorney." I didn't want anyone to know my business, and I was angry that she would say that to me, but I guess a part of me wasn't surprised because in her eyes it was always about Jeff.

A few days later, I tried to commit suicide by taking a small handful of my grandmother's prescription medicine and went to sleep. It was by the grace of God I woke up a few hours later. So, we called the detective, and I said it wasn't true, that I lied and they closed the case. However, the detective shared since I was a minor she was going to close the case in a way that the media couldn't get hold of it and Jeff went back to the halfway house. Not long after that he was partying and taking drugs when the halfway house did a surprise drug test. He knew he wasn't going to pass so he jumped out of the window and not long afterward we prepared to leave.

I was picked up from school early and told that we were going to Massachusetts. My son was in the car already along with my sisters. It wasn't until we were on the highway for a while that Jeff turned back to me and said we weren't going to Massachusetts but back to California. He said it with a smile on his face, and I wanted to cry. All I kept thinking was that I'd lost any chance to be happy. Carson was a good person, and although I wasn't in love with him, I had much love for him. I did, however, have a chance to tell him that I was pregnant before leaving. I couldn't get a response from him until later. I knew it was wrong to mislead Carson knowing he wasn't the father, but since Henry was going to college I didn't think he would've stayed in contact with me had I told him the truth.

After a day on the road, I got over it. Laura and Jeff knew that I was pregnant. I was only 16 years old at the time, and they both seemed ok with it. I think Jeff was ok until I gave birth, his words to me were, "I thought she was mine until you had her because the dates didn't add up." In a way, I thought to have a child by someone else meant the father would be in the picture, and things would change, but they didn't. I guess I was just naïve.

We arrived back in California for the second time. This time we stayed at a motel in Los Angeles. While there, I was admitted to the hospital for a couple of days because of a kidney infection. The day I was discharged my mother came to pick me up, and I noticed there was no Jeff. I asked where he was and she said he got arrested for a warrant in Connecticut. I thought we would go back to Connecticut and I wasn't the only one thrilled. When we got to the motel room, we began looking at the map to see which way we were going to drive back to Connecticut. I was so excited, but I contained it. We then begin to pack everything away, and Laura became distracted for a moment and started watching television. We heard a knock on the door, and we looked at each other. When she opened the door, we both were shocked. It was Jeff, and he said that they let him go. I thought, Dang! Why, why, why? He started saying how he had already begun preparing mentally for extradition back to Connecticut.

As time went on the sexual abuse started again. It's weird thinking about it now because Jeff never hit me while I was pregnant. Being pregnant was a temporary break from all violence. I could hear him yelling at Laura one night. I don't know what he was yelling about because I was asleep. What caught my ear was when he told Laura to shut up before you wake her (talking about me) up. I lay still on the bed because I didn't want him to know that I was already awake. I heard her sniffing as if she was crying and I just began praying, "Please Lord don't let her have any bruises on her face. I didn't want the children to see her that way." It pretty much calmed down after that. Jeff became friends with some guy and his wife that lived at the motel also, and it wasn't long before accusations were going around that Jeff was having sex with her.

We moved into our first apartment in Long Beach, California on Bennet St. This would be the place that the physical abuse would become more frequent. It was all right in the beginning, and then he began yelling at every little thing. For example, he got upset one time because Laura braided my son's hair and he didn't want it braided. So she had to take it a loose, or he would yell at my son telling him to stop crying. Then one night while giving my son his bath, my water broke. I took my son out of the tub and got him dressed, and Laura drove me to the hospital. I thought this one was going to be like when I had my son Jack, but boy was I wrong. The contractions started striking me, and I kept telling Laura to get the nurse. When the nurse finally came and checked me, they rushed me to the delivery room. They kept saying to push then stop. Later I was told that my baby girl was born with the umbilical cord wrapped around her head in a knot. I thanked God that she was alive and everything was good with her. She had beautiful curly hair and chubby cheeks that you just wanted to pinch. I named her Jamie. I didn't have many clothes for her because I wasn't working and didn't have any income coming in at 17 years old. My mom was getting cash assistance, and she would get pampers for Jamie.

CHAPTER 10
DECISION AND CONSEQUENCES

I couldn't wait to turn 18, so I could get my own money. That was all I thought about; the things I wanted to buy. As the time came near to my 18th birthday, I started thinking I should just get the money from cash assistance and take my son and daughter back to Connecticut.

I begin talking to my Aunt Octavia and telling her I was thinking of going back on my 18th birthday and she started saying that she wanted to come to California. I told her I would wait for her to come down and if she decided to return to Connecticut, I would go back with her. I told her not to say anything to Jeff. Even so, he came to me and said I heard that when you turn 18 years old that you were leaving and going back to Connecticut. I don't know why she told him. I just said no, I told her I was thinking about it. Plans ruined! I kept thinking he was never going to let me leave. Aunt Octavia came, and she brought my two cousins along with her, but failed to tell us that she didn't tell their father (who was also abusive to her).

While she was there, I began writing a journal about how I felt and what was going on with Jeff. One day I came in from the store with my mother and Aunt Octavia was in the living room, and she looked like she was crying. She said the kid's father was in California and on his way to the house. He wanted them to go back to Connecticut. Laura went in the bedroom with Jeff. I don't know what was said, but when she came out, she said, "Jeff wants you," and she was looking down. I was scared to go, but I didn't have a choice. As soon as I went in the room, POW! Slapped in the face. He followed with questions like "What have you been telling Octavia about me?" I said nothing, and he hit me again saying, "Why is she saying you told her things that have been going on in this house?" I knew he was talking about him raping me. I answered that I didn't know and just then, someone knocked on the door, and he told me to go in the room.

I started thinking Aunt Octavia must have read my journal. I didn't know why she would tell him. I don't know if it was loyalty to him or what, all I knew was to never confide in her about anything. As I was in my room, Octavia went outside to talk to her children's father, and she ended up packing their things and leaving. I stayed in my room and didn't say anything to her. When she said goodbye I just waved because I had absolutely nothing to say to her. I just started praying that Jeff didn't come in my room and start hitting me. The Lord answered my prayer because he didn't come in my room, at least not that day.

A couple of months later (by this time I was 18 years old) he called me in the living room in the middle of the night while everyone was asleep. As I walked in the living room, I was praying everything was going to be ok. He began saying how upset he was that I had gotten pregnant by someone else while he was in jail and that Jamie should've been his. He went on to say, "Sometimes I feel like tying up your feet and hands and putting you in a tub of water." I got scared, but that was nothing compared to what he said next. He went on, "You know I thought about shooting you up with heroin, but I didn't want to give you too little and you don't feel anything and I didn't want to give you too much, and you overdosed." My body was shaking, and all I could think was God please don't let him kill me. After a little while, he had sex with me, and I went back to bed.

I know that when some people read this, they will wonder why Laura didn't stop this or why did she care more for Jeff than her children? My answer is Laura was going through the abuse too, physically and mentally. Today, I have forgiven Laura I am very close to her. I've also forgiven my abuser too, but there isn't much communication between us. I feel I have healed past this by the grace of God. Here are a couple of examples of Jeff abuse to Laura.

Jeff would bring all kinds of women in the house even while Laura was home. He didn't care that she was the mother of his children. The women would sometimes spend the night, and you could hear them having sex in the living room. Two people come to mind as I type, Angelina, who was a friend of a neighbor and one who came over often. Well, one-day Laura must have gotten tired of it and told Angelina she wanted her out of her house. I guess she didn't think my mom was going to do anything, and responded, yea ok and went back in the bedroom (yes, she went back into Laura's bedroom with Jeff). It was early afternoon when she had told her to leave, the evening came, and Angelina was still in there. My mother said to me, "If anything happens call 911." I didn't know what she was about to do. She then came out of the kitchen with a big pot of boiling water and went into the bedroom. All I heard was, "Angelina I asked you nicely to leave…" and Angelina said. "Ok, Laura. I'm leaving now," and she did leave.

There was another situation that happened where I didn't understand why my mother didn't do anything. Tabatha, was someone that we knew from staying at a hotel in LA. She was living with her boyfriend there but came over one night, drank and had sex with Jeff. In the morning when I went to fix my daughter a bottle, the woman was laying on the couch half naked. When I went in the room, I heard my mother come out of her room, and I know she saw the woman lying there. However, she did nothing, and the lady left when she woke up.

Not long after that, my mother and I left to take the children to the park. It was my two children ages one and two, as well as my sisters who were three and four at the time. As we arrived at the corner just from the house, we saw all these sheriff officers in green jackets. I had a feeling they were there for Jeff. We went back to the house because my mother forgot something. We all went in, and not long afterward there was a bang on the door. When Jeff asked who it was, they said it was the police. When he opened the door, they rushed in with guns pointed at him asking to see his hands and then to put them behind his back. They then asked him his name, and after he told them, they announced a warrant for his arrest. When they handcuffed him and took him to jail, we didn't know why. Later that day Jeff called to see if we knew anything. He asked me if I had called the police on him because just before we left Connecticut, I told my grandmother what he was doing to me, and she called his parole officer who sent him back to jail. I guess Jeff thought that I had something to do with the situation, but it wasn't me. We later found out it was because he beat up the boyfriend of Tabatha, the woman from LA. It was so bad the guy thought he was being pistol-whipped, so they noted on the warrant that his hands were a deadly weapon.

Laura and I thought he was going to do some time. We were happy for a minute. Then we found out he was getting out and we were like dang. Why?! It seemed like every time Jeff went to jail or got arrested he came right back out. As I sit back and reflect on this, it's terrible to be happy for someone to be in jail because usually for other people it's a sad thing.

After his release, things went back to the way they were. After about six months, Jeff's sister Reese came to

California from Connecticut with her three children. They stayed with us until Jeff started complaining that she needed to get herself an apartment. Eventually, she found an apartment a couple of blocks away from us. Reese was coming over often, and of course, they would drink and get high. Every time Jeff drank I would get paranoid because I never knew what was going to happen; whether it was going to be a quiet night or if he was going to call me in the living room and bring up something old that happened so he could hit me.

I remember one particular night he called me in the living room after my mother went into the shower. He unplugged the telephone and was wrapping the cord around his hands as he told me something that Laura had told him I did. When he asked me about it I wanted to get his mind off of choking me, so I said you know I saw Reese and Laura talking about something. They were whispering every time I came in the room. He then asked if I heard what they were saying. I said no, and just then Laura came out of the bathroom. Jeff went to the back, and all I heard was Laura gasping for air. I began crying and thinking about what I had done. I didn't want her to get choked either. He then let her go in the bedroom but came in the living room and began hitting me. I just prayed that he didn't kill me. All the children were in their beds asleep. The next day I had a black eye and a swollen jaw. I stayed in my room wondering when it was going to end and although the children saw the bruises they never spoke about it. Jeff disciplined the children, but it didn't turn into abuse until years later. Reese came over and saw my face as I was coming out of the bathroom. She didn't say anything but left. Five minutes later the phone line in my room rang. What she called to ask was I ok, and I told her yes. Then she said, "Y'all better be careful over there." After a while, Reese moved to Compton, California because she stabbed someone in her apartment that tried to rape her. A few months later she moved back to the East coast. Not long after Reese left, Laura's Section 8 came through, so we moved to a house in the suburbs.

Everything was going fine until I started waking up to Jeff slapping me because he thought I was acting like I was sleep. The rule was when he turned off the television in the living room, I had to come to him. I began buying no-doze and taking them to keep me awake. After a while, that didn't work, and I found myself waking up to him hitting me again. Eventually, I started smoking weed with Jeff and Laura. It's sad to say that those were good times; smoking weed and playing spades (shaking my head). I guess because there was no yelling or arguing at that time is what made it good. My sister jokes around now saying I remember the time when you, mommy, and father played spades and smoked weed.

I began taking computer classes which weren't far from the house. I graduated and started doing temp work; it wasn't long before the abuse began again. I felt at times like my mother disliked me because of a comment she once made. She said to me one day, "You and Jeff act like high school kids. He's playing around with you, and you are laughing and playing around back with him." I started to get a little depressed because I was doing what I needed to do to keep from being beat. After so many years of going through the motions and acting like we were a typical family (with a secret everyone knew), I guess I just went with the flow of everything.

Laura and I started taking the kids to the park on the weekends, we would talk about things we wanted to do, or sometimes we just talked about Jeff. One time Laura said to me that Jeff was thinking about asking me to get a shotgun for him since he can't do it with his record. I thought he didn't need a gun in the house, but she came out and said what I was thinking. I replied, "I hope he doesn't ask me because he doesn't need it." A couple of weeks went by before Jeff said to me that he wanted me to get a shotgun for him. All I could say was ok and pray that he would change his mind, but he didn't. The following month he asked me to get the shotgun. We went to the gun store, I filled out the application, everything cleared, and I went back with the money to buy it. Everything was calm for a minute. Laura and I became more involved with the PTA at the kids' school.

Jeff and my mother began using crack. It started as a weekend thing and progressed over time. One night they were getting high, I guess he was expecting me to come in the living room and I was asleep. He was yelling at Laura that morning. I started thinking, "I'm next..." Just as I thought it Laura came out of her room and said, "Jeff wants you." As soon as I walked in the room to see what he wanted, Slap! He then began yelling, asking, why I didn't come in the living room. I told him I fell asleep and he asked me why was I lying. When I told him I'm not, he went and got the gun, cocked it, and pointed at me. I said whatever I thought he wanted to hear even if it meant telling a lie. Praying in my mind, I begged: "Please God don't let him shoot me." He then told me to leave, and I thought what if he shot me as I went to my room. Tears rolled down my face. I tried to put a smile on my face so the children wouldn't see I was crying. I kept saying to myself "Why is this happening to me and why won't he get rid of the gun?"

I would sleep during the day so that I could stay up at night. I was too afraid of what might happen if I fell asleep again. Well, after taking no-doze for a while it was like taking candy it stopped working. I began getting hit again for not waking up. After a while I got into the habit of not sleeping through the night, and always questioned what I did to deserve all of this.

It wasn't long before I became pregnant with my third child. I decided to keep the baby because I knew I wouldn't get hit while I was pregnant. It took some time before I told anyone. While at the park one day, the kids were playing and Laura and I were sitting on the bench. She said to me, "Jeff thinks you're pregnant." I replied,

"What did you say?" Laura said, "I told him to ask you." She didn't say anything to me about it, that's when I told her that he was right and I was pregnant. By then I was about three months. I thought there would be at least six months without any physical violence. Laura and I continued to get more involved in the school PTA carnivals, fundraisers, and candy sales.

Jeff wasn't working consistently. I slowly started buying things for the baby around my 8th month. I put together the crib, started buying more clothes and blankets. Then not long after that, Laura and I were walking to pick the children up from school. I had contractions to the point where I had to stop every few minutes (well it may have been a little shorter, but it felt like a few minutes). We finally got to the school and the principal saw us and asked was everything ok. I said yes, but then Laura said I was having contractions. So, the principal had me sit down while she had someone bring the children to us. She kept asking me did I want her to call the ambulance. I replied no. After I made it home, I couldn't take the pain anymore so Laura called 911 and I went to the nearest hospital because the paramedics didn't want to take any chances.

After I was admitted, I received an epidural. Jeff met us at the hospital. After the epidural kicked in the contractions weren't so bad. Not long after it was time to deliver. I thought I would be moved to another room to deliver the baby, but they removed a section of the bed and I delivered right there in the room. After checking my baby's vitals, they transported me to the hospital where I was supposed to have my baby. There I was told that my baby girl had jaundice. They also took blood samples and said that she needed a blood transfusion. I stayed at the hospital when I could but yearned for her to be home with me.

I named her Jill; I was finally able to bring her home after being in the hospital a week. I held her, played with her and showed her to the other children. Because of the light therapy she needed from being jaundiced, she was darker than my other children, but it didn't make much difference to me for I loved her just as much as the others. Come to think of it; she was the only child that had a crib, a playpen, and professional baby pictures. It wasn't long before everything went back to the dysfunction of me popping no-doze to stay awake so I could be alert for my cue of the television being turned off.

One the weekends Laura and I would take the kids to the park. Those were relaxing times. Also, we would talk about going to Connecticut or what female Jeff was with the night before. We never spoke about what Jeff was doing to me as far as the sexual abuse, and I never brought it up. I guess I didn't talk about it because I didn't know how to approach her with it. Half of the stuff went on while she was asleep, she didn't know anything happened until I got pregnant, and she never saw boys come to the house or me going out with anyone. Those were also the times she would ask if I was pregnant or tell me what assumptions Jeff had told her he had about me.

The rest of the kids were close friends with the children across the street from us. Around the holidays, they would make egg rolls from scratch and give them to us, and we would give them chocolates and snacks. We would also give our mail lady bottled water on hot days.

One day she delivered mail to us, and she had a black eye. She looked so down I wanted to say girl I know how you feel; I took the mail but said nothing. Thinking about domestic violence in general, advocacy has come a long way from the 70s. But there's still a hush about it. Most people don't speak out unless they hear another person's story. You never know what the person next to you at church, work, or school has been through until she tells you.

Jeff and Laura found out that the owner of the house we were renting had lost it to foreclosure. The money we were giving him for rent he was using for other things besides the mortgage. Told we had to move, my mother took the owner to court and won. We moved from an area that had a majority Caucasians to a more urban area. It was still a house, but bigger. After some time, we adjusted. Everything worked out, and the kids made new friends.

Once settled at our new place, Jeff and Laura would get high, but only on the weekends in the beginning. Laura would work for a temp agency when jobs were available, but it wasn't long before Laura became addicted to crack. One day she told me she was going to the mall to return some things. I went with her knowing that stealing was going to be involved, but for some reason, I wanted to go. We went and took the children with us. Well, we got caught and had to call Jeff to pick up the kids. The cops put us in a holding cell. I was praying that they would let us out, mainly me because at the time I already had a warrant for failure to appear for a previous shoplifting charge. I just prayed, "Lord if you allow me to get out I will not do this again." About five minutes later the officer came to the cell we were in and said, "I'm going to release you and give you a ticket to appear in court." I thought he was only talking to Laura, so I said, "Me too?" He said, "Yes, I will give you another court date for the warrant." I thanked God, and I never stole again after that day.

I began contacting Mike again, and I sent him Christmas gifts. We talked about me moving back to Connecticut and him and I having a baby, it would be our 1st child together. As time went, it became more of a dream than a reality. Before I knew it, a year had passed, and Mike was talking to someone else. I was hurt, but I still called him occasionally and sent him money at times (at the time I was getting cash and food stamps) to pay for his phone bill. Whatever he asked for and if I had the money I just did it. I guess the real reason was I still had hope that he and I would be together. Things were stressful for me at that time. Everything started to build up; the pressure of always being awake when Jeff turned the television off. A couple of times I went in the living room, and he was having sex with some female. I was glad and hoping she stayed until the morning, which they usually did. My mother doing her drug thing and the physical abuse of us both was still going on.

Jeff's brother came to California and stayed with us for a little while. One night Jeff knew Laura was getting high and they started arguing. I began praying with tears coming down, "Lord, please don't let him kill her." She was screaming while he was hitting her in the bathroom. My sister Jane came and knocked on my door. I opened it, and she said she was going to call 911 because couldn't take it anymore. I agreed. She dialed the number then hung up. They called back, and Jeff let Laura out of the bathroom to answer the phone. The dispatcher kept her on the phone until the police got there. When the police arrived, they arrested Jeff and took pictures of the bathroom as well as Laura's face. Blood was everywhere, on the floor, the wall and her face. Later she told me that he had hit her in the face with the lid from the toilet tank. I couldn't believe he did that to her. The next morning when he was getting out of jail, Laura made the same remark from before something about Jeff and me playing around like high school kids. I told her that's not how it was. Our situation had been going on for so long I just did things so I wouldn't get hit or make the situation worse. "I don't want him touching me," I told her.

She then told me that Jeff told her I wanted to have sex with him, he didn't force me! I asked if she believed him and she said yes. I told her then I was going to try and leave to go to Connecticut. I don't know if Laura turned a blind eye to the point where she didn't believe it was happening or didn't want to accept it. I don't know the reasons for her responses when it came to the sexual abuse. So much was going through my mind then. Why would my mother believe that? How could she think I wanted him when it started at the age of five? I didn't know what sex was! I know I didn't want him then. Did she think because I was now older I wanted him? That wasn't the case because I cried every time he had sex with me from the age of five until that day.

I called my cousin Irene to see if she could help me with getting tickets for my children and me to return to Connecticut. She said she would support my decision, just let her know how much and when. I wasn't working at the time and was receiving cash assistance and food stamps. So, I priced the tickets for us to travel one way to Connecticut. I called Irene back and told her I would need help and told her the day I wanted to leave. She said ok, but I felt that she didn't want to do it. I told Laura I was leaving when I got my cash, and of course, she told Jeff. He came to me and said your mother said that you're moving. "Yep" I replied, but when the day came my cousin didn't answer her phone and wouldn't return my calls. So, I thought to myself that I had to get the tickets one by one. I got mine first and figured that I could get two kids tickets at a time, but it seemed like things kept coming up. Before I knew it, almost a year had gone by, but during that time I was dealing with my mother's drug addiction on top of the abuse. I had to go! One particular month after I received my money, I paid my bills for the month and told Laura that I was leaving but coming back. She was high that I don't think she understood what I said. I went to the salon. It was like my son knew because he asked if he could come with me, which wasn't normal. I told him no and left. I went to the salon, then bought a pair of pants, a t-shirt, and some underwear, I didn't want my family to see how run down I looked. I also purchased a travel kit that had toothpaste, deodorant, and powder. I then went to the Greyhound bus station, I had to use the ticket I had before it expired and I didn't have the money to get my children tickets. I was coming back, but I just had to leave. Laura was on drugs, Jeff began hitting me more frequently, and I just didn't know what else to do. I called my cousin Irene as well as my grandmother and told them I was on my way there. They both told me Laura called and asked them if I had got in touch with them. I explained that I had told Laura and maybe she didn't understand what I was saying. I didn't call Laura until I got to Connecticut and Jeff asked when I was coming back. I told him I didn't know. Then Jeff shared my case worker called from welfare and wanted me to call her back. I spoke to my kids, my daughter Jamie kept asking why I didn't take her with me. I felt so hurt. Jeff and Laura told me she cried the whole time and wouldn't eat. I wasn't thinking wisely. I knew I was going back and planned to go just to pick up my children and return to Connecticut, however, that didn't happen. As I'm writing this I am thinking; I had one paid ticket why couldn't I take all my cash aid and leave with my children? Why didn't I do what would've resulted in fewer years of abuse? I think part of the reason was that my mother and I were very close and I was waiting for her to come with me. I was the only one there for her in her addiction. But, I didn't know that she would never leave.

I was deeply depressed, so I left my grandmother's house and went to visit with family and old friends. On the way, back to my grandmother's house, I met a guy named Ronnie. He was tall, skinny and light brown complexion. We talked for a couple of hours, and for a few moments, I forgot about my problems. He had an apartment, things were going fast between us, and shortly after we met, I would go to his house every night. I told him my situation, and he said he wanted me to stay with him. I told him I couldn't because I had to go back and get my children. We started talking about being and living together. No, we hadn't been together long just a few weeks. As I think about it now, I shake my head and ask myself what was I thinking at the time. I guess it was hearing someone say it was going to be ok and that they cared and/or said they cared.

My Aunt Pricilla paid for my ticket after about a week of Jeff and Laura calling asking when was I coming back. I wasn't looking forward to going back and dealing with Jeff. I only wanted to see my children and siblings. On the road back to California, depression began to set in as I thought about how hard he was going to make it for me to leave. I didn't eat the whole time while traveling. I got to California, and I gave all my kids and siblings a hug and promised Jamie that I would never leave her again. I was so skinny and began to shiver for two days. I went to the emergency room; the doctor said I needed to take iron pills and that I was pregnant, again. The doctor said I was so skinny that he could feel the fetus just by touching my stomach I told him I would eat right and see the doctor.

I called Ronnie and told him but confessed it wasn't his because the doctor told me I was four months pregnant with my 4th child. He still wanted us to be together, but it seemed like things weren't going right for me to leave. I hardly had any money to save and go back home. I went back into depression because I knew Ronnie was seeing someone else. Then, one day it was confirmed when he answered the phone, and I heard a female voice in the background. I asked him about it he said she's just a friend, but if I didn't want it to turn into something else I need to hurry back. I was hurt and called him less. I kept the baby, began to see a doctor regularly and one day decided to attend church. The kids participated with children's church so I could enjoy the service. The pastor did an altar call, and I went to the front and knelt there. As I was on my knees praying, thanking God, and telling Him I give it all to Him, I felt this warm sensation over my face and a weight lifted from my back. As I continued praying I could hear the pastor say someone come minister to this young lady over here. I then felt warm hands on my back, and all I could do was thank God. That moment was my first real encounter with the presence of the Lord. Although my grandmother taught me how to pray, I never felt anything like that before. Light and overwhelmed with tears of joy that God had visited me in that way.

I continued going to that church, and there we found out one of the member's kids and ours (mine & Laura's) went to the same school. Our families became friends, and our relationship grew to the point of looking out for each other's children while going to school, etc.

I attended the Community Worship Center frequently, stayed in my word and fasted to strengthen my relationship with God. Since I was pregnant, I wasn't fasting from food but using my time differently instead of watching television. I listened to gospel music or would meditate for a few hours on the days that Jeff was at work. The Lord began showing me how to anoint and pray over the house inside and out. The time was quickly approaching for my baby girl to arrive. I made sure I had Pampers, wipes, baby lotion and baby wash, some onesies, t-shirts and a couple of outfits. Then it was time to have her at the hospital with no epidural.

Jeff was there in the room with me as he was present for the births of the other children (except with Jamie).

When the doctor told me my baby girl was healthy, I thanked God. I decided to name her Jem because after all the stress I went through in my pregnancy and not having prenatal care the first four months, her coming into this world healthy was precious to me. I was grateful that although my life up that point was stressful, I had precious and healthy children. Jem came home, and all the kids wanted to hold her and play as they did with all their siblings. I read books to her as I did with the previous children.

CHAPTER 11
WILL I EVER LEAVE

Jem was a few months old, and Jeff started working for a temp agency. The job hired him permanently, and he acted like he worked all his life, always complaining. I remember one time Jeff started yelling at me about how I cleaned and said he purposely put a piece of paper behind the toilet to see if anyone was going to pick it up. I started thinking, why would he put it behind the toilet and how long did he wait before saying anything? We met a lady and her children that lived in the building behind our house. Her name was Sutaria, and she would come over to the house on Jeff's days off to drink, hang out and bring her children to play. Sutaria tried her best to befriend my mother, but I knew it was phony. She didn't like either of us, and the feeling was mutual.

As time went on, we limited our socializing with people. There was a lady that lived across the street from us, Laura knew her, and she came over one day. She began talking about the Bible which I loved to do. While talking, she came out and said she was born with a black veil. Laura and I looked at each other, now I knew about people being born with a veil which is an extra layer of skin over the face, but I didn't know there were colors. I just didn't feel comfortable around her; she continued talking about what some people in her family would do to get back at people. I thought, how nasty when I heard some of the things she was saying. When she left, Laura said, "I knew there was something wrong with her because she has a picture on the wall in her apartment that looks like it was taken in the early 1900s with some man and a little girl. She said the little girl was her and I know she's not older than me!" After my mother told me that, I got my oil and began anointing and praying over everything from the front porch to the back. I didn't want any demonic spirits to attach itself to anything or anyone in the house. I just felt she dealt with evil whether she knew it or not.

I developed an interest in owning my own business, so I enrolled in a 12-week program to start one and learned the step by step guideline on how to do a business plan. I wanted to open a video store. It's funny because one day I was talking to the clerk from the local video store and I told her of my aspirations to own one. In support of what I told her she gave me information about where to purchase permits, video supplies, as well as movies. I know that was nobody but God. While taking the class, I met some interesting people; a young lady who was opening a salon, an older woman (pastor) who was starting a nonprofit business and a guy who was in the military trying to patent a product. The lady pastor and I got along great. She would come over to the house when Jeff was at work. Sometimes I felt like one of the kids having people over when he was at work then rushing them to leave before he came home. Then there were times I would go over to her house, but I wouldn't stay long.

One evening while she was over and my mother and I were discussing the Bible just enjoying ourselves, my youngest sister (Janice) at the time (because Laura had another baby) came in the living room with half her face swollen. We asked her what happened and she said nothing she had just woken up. We went into the bedroom and noticed that there was no sheet on her mattress. My friend stated it might have come from the mattress; half of my little sister's face had swollen up like a balloon. After we prayed over her, the swelling went down (the power of prayer). Later we found out she was allergic to the material of the mattress. Not long after, Laura and I found out my pastor friend had lost her son to violence; we saw her less and less until there was no more communication.

I completed my business plan for my video store and was supposed to get a microloan of $2500 once the program approved my business plan. The 1st time it was denied because I submitted it not typed. The 2nd time it was denied because a different person had the position of approving loans and she stated I had to change some things around. I didn't get a 3rd time because they had no one to approve loans at the time, so I just put it down ile and ventured out doing different things.

There was a talent show at my church, so I went to my sister Jane and asked her to be in the talent show with me. There were no auditions as long as you had a desire, which was their motto, we could participate. I was very active in church when able. Of course, I had to do something for her, she wanted me to take a picture with her, and she had to pick out the outfit we wore. I didn't like taking pictures (even in my 20s), and she knew it, but because I wanted us to be in the talent show, I agreed. We had fun participating.

I had a favorite gospel jazz CD that I listened to regularly. I also wrote two gospel songs that God gave to me. Since I knew the choir director, I thought we were friends, and he was a real man of God, so I shared my lyrics with him. I asked if he would come up with the music. After about a week he came to me and said he couldn't find any music for the lyrics I gave him. Sadly, years later he would use my songs on his CD Album. I received no recognition or compensation. It's sad when you can't trust someone in the body of Christ. When I found out what he did, I was so shocked. I found a way to contact him online years after I left my abuser to ask him about it but never received a response. From that experience, I learned never to trust anyone with something like that again. I just stayed in my word, watched Christian television and listened to gospel music. Occasionally, I would do little things here and there for the video store that I wanted to open as I dealt with continued abuse.

My mother was still there with me and would flee the abuse from time to time. However, she would come back, and Jeff would continue to abuse her as well.

Laura began to use crack again, but this time, the addiction was out of control. She would leave for days at a time and steal from me.

Although she was addicted, I never turned my back on her. She was my mother despite what I went through as a child and part of my adult life. I had to be there for her. My sisters would try and keep her in the house or on days that Jeff was at work they would go looking for her telling drug dealers not to sell to her. I was taking care of the children while all this was going on. During this time, my sister under me (Jane) was around 14, and there were eight children in the house. We never discussed the abuse at any time except for Jane occasionally would say how nasty it was that I was having sex with Laura boyfriend. I was hurt, and part of me wanted to tell her everything, but instead, I just kept telling her she didn't know everything. Her response was it didn't matter.

I began participating more in church activities. It seemed like the more I did it; the more Jeff became abusive towards me. He said to me one day why are you always doing stuff for the church. You do more at church then you do at home and out of nowhere POW! A slap in the face, then he put his hands around my neck. My thoughts were why me and I realized he was hitting me more than my mother. After this incident, I tried to commit suicide for the 2nd time by taking prescription medication I had for my throat. I took a small handful and went to sleep wishing I didn't wake up again. However, by God's grace, I woke up. I couldn't speak up because I was afraid he would kill me and I was terrified to leave. I knew his capabilities! I was trapped and needed a way of escape. I used to say, "Lord, when is Jeff going to die?" I wanted the abuse to stop, and death seemed to be the only way.

I questioned why I seemed to get it worse than my mother. Not that she deserved to get beat, but it was an honest question of how I felt at times. Eventually, Jeff began to ask me to marry him. Yes, he wanted to marry his common-law wife's daughter and believed he should've made me do it a long time ago. Occasionally Jeff and I went to the casinos in Las Vegas but it had been a minute since going, I guess he wanted to get married the next time we went. THANK GOD it never happened!

I was at a point where I felt like I wanted to date. Due to my circumstances, dating was something I rarely did while in California. Thinking about it now, I wish I had a father figure in my life to teach or show me how a real man should treat me. My biological father was addicted to drugs all of my childhood, and I have a couple of good memories. When I was little, don't remember my exact age at the time, I had on a pink dress , and he bought me a strawberry ice cream cone. Another time was when I was older about 13 years old I was staying at my aunt house, and he brought me a whole watermelon and took me to Bradlees Department Store to buy me some clothes. I cherish those memories now since he is no longer living.

I liked looking at wedding magazines, and Jeff felt since I had the magazines I wanted to marry him. He didn't know I was just fantasizing about marrying someone else and started meeting people while Jeff was at work. Those I met didn't know of my abuse, but they knew who he was and that he was violent. I knew I couldn't be in a real relationship and I made sure they understood that it was just a friendship. Now I know, some may be thinking while reading this was any sex involved. To answer the question, yes, at times it was. I must clarify that I didn't have sex with every guy I met. There was one guy I really liked named Joe. He would be the last person I dated before leaving California. He was tall, caramel complexion and a thin build. I always went to his house while Jeff was at work. It's funny because he had a dog (which I don't like animals) but his dog and I got along just fine. I got caught up in my feelings and didn't want him with anyone else. If I called him and he was busy, I would have an attitude. I didn't believe what he told me when I first met him, but like Maya Angelou said, "When people show you who they are, believe them." He told me he had children all over the United States with different women. I thought, yeah right until I started seeing him with them.

You would think when I saw this I should've left him alone, but no I kept seeing him knowing he was screwing other people. I guess I just wanted to feel loved, and if I spent time with him, to me it was love. I didn't know my self-worth then; I didn't realize that I was someone's gift. It's funny how sometimes you don't see things until after the situation, even if someone is trying to tell you or it's staring you right in the face.

After a few months, I found out I was pregnant again. Because of a promise that I made to God, I kept the baby. I told Jeff that I was pregnant with my 5th child, he asked what was I going to do, I said keep it. I knew it was Jeff's, so I stopped talking to Joe. As I got further along in my pregnancy, I started buying the baby some things. I already knew I was going to have a girl. I had a baby shower, and she was the only child whom I could have a baby shower. The physical abuse wasn't happening, not while I was pregnant anyway. The time finally came for me to have my baby girl and I didn't have anyone by my side this time. I stayed in the hospital two extra days because I told my doctor before I gave birth that I wanted my tubes tied. When it was time, the doctor came and stated that they were waiting for my insurance to approve it. After the 2nd day I was discharged from the hospital with no tubes tied, Laura told me it wasn't meant to happen.

CHAPTER 12
MY ESCAPE

The nurse came in and told me that I was being discharged. I was happy and unhappy at the same time. I was happy because I missed my family and wanted to see them (children, brothers, and sisters), I was unhappy because I knew things would go back to how they were. I came home, and all the children were around my new bundle of joy, Josephine. Laura was in prison for theft, and she was also having a baby girl (her 5th child by Jeff).

It wasn't long before the abuse continued with Jeff. I wanted out so bad, but I didn't have the money to leave. Looking back now, I think why couldn't I just save my money? Although I was getting state assistance, I could've saved a few bucks here and there. I guess I didn't think I would ever leave, until one day while sitting in the living room watching television with my sister, the voice of the Lord that said, "Take the kids and leave." At first, my spirit answered, "Lord is that you?" I paused and heard nothing. So I said, "Lord if that's you then make a way that I will have money to leave." I turned to my sister and said the Lord just told me to take the kids and go. She asked, "What are you going to do and where are you going to go?" I didn't know without money. Just then my eldest daughter overheard our conversation and said, "I just got my cheerleading uniform. I can see if I can return it and get the money back?" I asked, "How much?" She stated, "$35.00." I agreed, and while she went to the school, which was at the end of the block, I called Greyhound to price tickets to other towns in California. I wanted to go far so I could have some time to think. I had left a few times before but always stayed close to Laura and Jeff. The one place that kept coming to mind was Riverside, California.

My daughter came back with the money, my two sisters and I began talking about how much we're going to miss each other. While sitting in the living room chair, the Lord said, "Hurry up and leave he will be home soon, and then you won't ever leave." I called the cab and me, and my five children (Jack, Jamie, Jill, Jem, and Josephine) with two huge suitcases and a couple of bags got in a cab. It was October of 2000 that I left for the last time. As I think back, I don't know how I got the money for the cab. I told my sisters and brother I loved them and that I would call them from my cell phone. We got to Greyhound, and with the money, I was able to buy one-way tickets for one adult and four children to Riverside, California and had $5.00 left over. God is oh so Good!

Once we got on the road for a while, I called my sister Jane to see what was going on. She said she called and told Jeff that I left; he was on his way home at the time. I was relieved because we were out of Long Beach, California. I didn't know how far Riverside was, but the sun was out when we left, and it was 9:00 pm when we arrived.

CHAPTER 13
GOD WILL MAKE A WAY

The journey to freedom began and to prepare; I called a domestic violence shelter before I left the house. I was so hurt when the lady told me the shelter in the area would only take me if I had bruises. I wanted to cry but I couldn't in front of my children. I told her that I didn't have any bruises and asked if there were any other shelters that my children and I could go to for the night. She then gave me an address of another shelter, so I tried to get a cab. None would take me, because it was me, my five children and our luggage. Just as I felt like giving up a small little taxi came, and the guy said, "I'll take you, where do you have to go?" I told him the address, and he said he knew where it was, but he didn't think they opened until November. I started praying for the Lord to please help me.

We got there, and he was right. I asked the cab driver if he knew of any other shelters, but he didn't. He told me to keep the $5.00 and offered to buy the children something to eat. He treated them to McDonald's, paid for one night at a hotel for us, said he would ask around and come back in the morning to let me know. He then helped me with my luggage to the room. While typing this part right here, it's amazing how God works and the people he uses to bless you abundantly.

I got the children ready for bed; I prayed that we didn't have to sleep on the street and that if we had to go to a shelter, it would be clean. The morning came, and the kids were watching television as I was trying to figure out what I would give my kids for breakfast. I knew that I was going to get my food stamps and cash soon, and that would last for a while, but first I had to get through the next couple of days.

There was a knock on the door, and it was the cab guy. He came with some food for the kids. He then said that he hadn't found anything yet and paid for another day. Although I was grateful for what he was doing, I felt helpless because I couldn't do anything. I was in a town where I knew no one or how to get around. I didn't know what type of person this cab driver was; I just prayed that he didn't expect anything physical in return and thanked God that wasn't the case. I told him that I would get my cash in a couple of days. The next morning, he took me to the county office because he stated I needed to transfer my case from Long Beach to Riverside and they may be able to help me.

After being there the whole day with the kids and the luggage, the cab driver rushed back and said he found a shelter for us in Corona. It's wasn't far, but we had to be there by a particular time to get in. We got there just in time, and yes it was clean. The only thing was we had to leave every morning and be back by 6:00 pm to get back in. We slept on mats. There were other people there with and without children.

We would go to the shopping center not far from the shelter and sit in the parking lot; I didn't know what to do. I felt terrible not just because we were at a shelter, but because we sat in a parking lot with our belongings all day. People came up to me giving us burgers from Burger King. I felt ashamed and to top it all off, I called my sister to see how everything was going and she told me that Jeff was going to look for me. I felt so depressed and disappointed I hung up the phone and wanted to cry. I guess it showed on my face because my son and oldest daughter did not argue or fight that day. Instead they joked around trying to put a smile on my face, and eventually, they did. I tried getting my mind off it by telling them when I got my money we were going to play laser tag. They were excited about that.

One day we were sitting in the parking lot, and I looked up towards the mountain. It was as if there was a door on that mountain that opened, and all I saw was a man in a white robe and felt this joyous feeling. I smiled and turned to my son, and he was smiling back at me. He said, "Yeah ma, I see it too." As I turned my head back, just that quick, it was gone.

The day came for me to pick up my cash off of my card, so I called someone who at the time lived in the next building from the house where Jeff lived. I told her what was going on and asked her not to say anything. I asked her if she could pick me up to take me to get my cash she said yes. She came and took me to a check cashing spot in L.A. County, but my card didn't work.

They were saying I needed another card because the magnetic strip wasn't working. I wanted to cry because it was a weekend, so it was back to the shelter with no money.

I found out when she got back to Long Beach she went and told Jeff what I told her but didn't tell him where I was. I took the kids to the park which was where everyone with kids from the shelter went. I still had my cell phone, so I called my sister, and while I was talking to her I heard my son saying mama, so I told my sister that I would call her back. I went to the swing area because that's where the kids were and to my surprise, my 12-year-old son was in the baby swing saying he was stuck. I asked why did he get in it and he replied to see if he fit. There were people from the shelter there trying to help get him out. Someone put Vaseline on his legs, he kept moving around, and he got out.

Monday came, and I called my caseworker to find out about my card. He tells me that I must first close my case in LA County and open a new case for Corona since I was in a different county. I thought, why God? I was disappointed and depressed; I took the kids and walked around. I didn't want to sit in the parking lot. Someone told me about a church that may help me because I had kids. I started thinking if I could get to Connecticut with my family, I'd be okay.

I went to the church and told them my situation and asked if they could help me get to Connecticut with my family. The woman there said they might not be able to pay for all the tickets, but maybe some and to ask family members if they can help. Also, call her in a couple of days because she had to talk to the pastor about it. I think my son was more hurt than me he started saying, "They're a church, right? I thought they're supposed to help people." I told him we didn't know what's going to happen and just wait.

I called my cousin and asked her if she could help me with a ticket back home. She said she would ask around. However, I knew that meant no one was going to help. After a couple of days went by I called the church back and was told to come in for a talk. I got my kids dressed, and we were on our way to the church. I guess they felt that I wasn't going to come because they called the shelter and told them to make sure they tell me to go there. I got to the church, and she asked if any family could help with the tickets. I told her no. She then said, "Well I have some good news, we had a special offering done just for you and were able to pay for your tickets and a church member offered to drive you and your family to the bus station." You don't know how bad I wanted to shout Thank You, Jesus! I was so happy, I cried. She stated that I would be leaving the next day and told me the time their person was coming to get my children and me. I told them when I got outside, and they were happy. I called a couple of my cousins and told them I was coming with my kids, and they were glad to hear that. The next day I was filled with excitement as I got the kids dressed and the family came to pick us up. As the children were helping with the bags by bringing them into Greyhound, the woman put something in my hand and said this is for you and the kids for food. I didn't look until we all got on the bus and I thanked her again. It was $65. We serve an awesome God.

The ride seemed quick, but maybe it was me wanting to be around my family that I hadn't seen in years. I kept in contact with my cousins along the way. I think my grandmother felt a way because usually when things happened she would be the first person I would call and I didn't this time. I'm not sure why I didn't call her, but I did when I got to my cousin's house. It was great seeing everyone. The word spread on the streets, my second day there someone that I used to talk to as a teen had come by, but I wasn't there. Later that night one of my daughters said, "Ma you need to go on a date." "No, I don't," I replied to her. Although I had been thinking I had never been on a date; not taken out to dinner or the movies, just hanging out at the guy's house even as a teen.

It was only a matter of time before Jeff started calling my grandmother's house and threatening whoever answered the phone. So finally, I answered his call, and he wanted to speak to the kids. So, I asked them if they wanted to talk to him and they all said yeah, and talked to him. When I got back on, he stated that whoever wanted to come back he was coming to get them. Now instead of telling him no because they weren't old enough to know what they wanted, I said ok so that he would stop calling. After I hung up, I asked everybody what they wanted to do, and everyone except my oldest daughter said they wanted to go back.

Looking back on this now I'm thinking why didn't I say no. That would have been enough for Jeff to leave me alone. All the children were in school; the school was calling me regarding my son having problems. He was mouthing off at the counselor, telling him, "Well my dad will be here in a couple of days to get me anyway." That was my son; he had a temper and spoke his mind at times, except, when he was around his father. The day came for Jeff to arrive and my uncle Albert gave my children their Christmas gifts because they were going back to California. When Jeff arrived that night, he acted as if he wanted to talk to me privately, but I didn't trust being alone with him. My uncle came outside with me and stayed until Jack 12, Jill 7, and Jem 5 and Jeff left. I felt hurt, but I couldn't show it and went back in the house. My cousins joked around with me to get me to laugh and get my mind off my children.

I began working, and my youngest stayed with my grandmother while I worked. She wasn't quite a year at that point. Some evenings my daughter (Jamie 10 years old) watched her as well. I thought Jeff would stop calling me, but he didn't.

A couple of weeks later I met this guy named Anthony he was about 5 ft. 7 inches tall, light-skinned and a little chubby. He wore glasses, had a job and a car. We started talking, and I wanted a relationship, but he wasn't ready for that. I began to spend the night at his house until my daughter called me crying and telling me my youngest daughter wouldn't go to sleep, and no one would help her. I went home but realized that my family would only help to a certain point. I tried to get my youngest daughter enrolled in daycare, but was put on a waiting list. Around that time, Jeff called saying I know you probably need help with the baby you should send her to me until you get on your feet. I regret allowing him to take any of my children. If I could have those days back, I would have said no and went into a domestic violence shelter. However, I agreed, so he flew to Connecticut to get my youngest daughter. All the children went back home, and it was just my oldest daughter and me. I figured I would give him what he wanted so he would stop contacting me. I regret letting him take them until this very day. Interestingly, he has a better relationship with them now than back at that time. Maybe it's because he's not the same person.

I still called my sisters and my children when I knew that their father was at work. After a while, I got served with a restraining order from Jeff. In it, he stated that I came to his house and threatened him with a gun. The judge granted the restraining order and later I was served again with custody papers. I had to go to court and was upset because legal aid in Connecticut told me I had to get representation from California since that's where the case was and California legal aid told me I had to get someone from Connecticut because that was where I resided. I was stressed, so I told Anthony about what I was going through, and he suggested that I call the sexual assault hotline. I did as he suggested and was assigned to a counselor who told me everything I needed to know. She said we needed a notarized letter stating everything that happened and must send it to the judge. I agreed.

We mailed the letter to the court, and I felt better having the opportunity to tell my side. However, I wanted to leave my grandmother's house because there was too much drama going on. After a couple of weeks, I received a letter from the judge stating the new court date and that I had to be there and I couldn't send any more correspondence to the court. I was so hurt and depressed because I didn't have the money for that. The court date had come and gone. Like I said earlier I would call my children and siblings when I knew Jeff was at work. I received another letter from the courts stating that I was allowed visitation and must pay child support for the maximum allowed for the state of California, over $900.00 per month. I was upset because I wasn't making that much money working. I went over to Anthony's house to tell him what was going on. All he could say was I've never heard of a woman paying child support.

I continued to keep in touch with my sisters and my children but didn't know Jane (my sister) and Jeff were telling my children not to talk to me because I didn't care about them and that's why I never visited them. After a while, Jill didn't want to talk to me anymore when I called then years later my other daughter Jem spoke to me less and less.

Looking back now I would've kept all the kids with me I just wanted Jeff to stop contacting me, and that's why I made a choice I regret so much. I had to have the house phone turned off because I couldn't afford it anymore. Jeff was still drinking from my understanding the verbal and physical abuse continued until my son and brother were 18. They began to fight back, but I don't know the details of what happened for this was shared with me long after it had happened. Jill was often hit for missing school and other things. As I heard this, I was hurting because there was a time that Jill felt I abandoned her by letting her go to Jeff. I asked Anthony if we could get an apartment together because at the time I couldn't afford it by myself. He kept saying no because he didn't feel the way I felt about him. That's when I went down the road of looking for love in all the wrong places.

I started talking to guys on chat lines, and I met a guy named Alex from Syracuse, New York who I would talk to all night. Laura was out of prison, and we would talk occasionally. I told her about the guy in Syracuse, and she seemed happy for me. After a couple of weeks, he wanted me to come to his house for the weekend, so I did. I liked it, and we started talking about if I was to move in with him what school my daughter would attend and how I could have my job transfer me. So, I went back to Connecticut and talked to my supervisor at the time, and she asked me if that was what I really wanted to do. I told her yes. I then spoke to my daughter and asked her how she felt about moving, and she was ok with it. I think she was ready to leave my grandmother's house too. I told Anthony that I was moving, but he didn't want me to go. I had to get out of my grandmother's house because there were too many people there and I didn't like how my grandmother was treating my daughter. Laura didn't want me to go either, but I made sure everyone had my cell phone number to stay in touch. I put in for my transfer at my job and asked them to mail my last check to Syracuse. (Looking back at all my past relationships I was looking to be loved and shown affection. When that didn't happen, I left the relationship with the mind to find another instead of taking care of myself). It was great in the beginning, but then I found out that he didn't have a job.

I applied for emergency food stamps and realized that I could've stayed in Connecticut. He started having his female friends come over and watch porn. I was still talking to Anthony while I was there and he wanted me to come back. I told him I wanted a relationship and us to move in together. I still had feelings for him, he agreed, so that next day I told the guy from Syracuse that as soon as my check came, I was going back to

Connecticut. At first, he said ok; then a big snow storm came that lasted for three days. After the storm my check came, I cashed it and told him I was leaving that next morning. He started asking if there was something he could do to make me change my mind. I said no. I got to Greyhound and didn't have enough for my tickets, so I had to call my aunt Pricilla, and she helped me get back.

When I got back to Connecticut, I reapplied for cash and food stamps and immediately began looking for an apartment because Anthony agreed for us to move in together and split everything. I kept getting turned down because of my credit. Then finally I found a 2-bedroom apartment for $570.00 a month. I called the owners, and they began telling me about the apartment and asked when I could look at it. I then asked if they go by credit and she stated, "No we go by how we feel when we meet you. Why do you ask?" I then told her that my credit wasn't that good and she told me don't worry about that. I went to see the apartment, it was nice, and all the rooms were so big. I was excited when I met the lady, and I spoke with her husband showing him the income for Anthony and me.

A couple of days later I received a call telling me I got the apartment and how much they required for the security deposit. I told the landlord I couldn't pay all the security deposit, so he added $100 to the rent every month until it was paid off. I was so excited to call Anthony and tell him we got the apartment. He had some furniture in storage, but because my daughter didn't have a bed and I didn't want her to sleep on the floor, I told her she had to stay at my grandmother house until I got her bed. Getting one for her didn't take a long time. I purchased a blow-up mattress. Anthony and I split the rent and the utilities. I was happy because this was my 1st official apartment on my own. Anthony and I broke up after a year because I caught him cheating more than once. Also, he was verbally abusive, and I couldn't deal with it anymore. After Anthony and I broke up, I went to church more got involved with my daughter (Jamie) school activities and became Co-PTA president for a little while (a lot of work that I didn't expect). Flashes of my abuse would come to my mind, but I would write down how I felt and prayed to God to make me whole. One time, God told me to call Jeff and pray for him, which took a couple of days to obey. I had to forgive him completely so all the anger, hatred and hurt I had for him could go away. Since I asked God to take it, the best way for Him to do that was for me to pray for Jeff. I called him, and he allowed me to pray do what God commanded. Now, I don't trust him, and although today we both have changed, I will never put myself in a position to be alone with him. He never asked me to forgive him nor do I ever expect to hear him ask me. My praying for him was God's final way of me breaking free from all I endured through the years.

You may wonder where my children are today and how is my relationship with them. My children are all in

California with their father except for my daughter (Jamie currently 28) and my son (Jack now 30) who visits me in New York occasionally. Laura lives with a roommate, goes to church and stays in her word. She does go and see my sisters and brother at Jeff house from time to time. My relationship with Laura is very close, and we talk almost every day on the phone. My relationship with my other daughters I pray will improve in time. I'm currently married and reside in New York we have a son together. I work for a domestic violence organization helping women every day.

Looking over my life in its entirety brings what if questions to mind such as,

1. What if I had told my grandmother sooner?
2. What if I would have researched domestic violence more to find out about shelters?
3. Why didn't family reach out to me and try to help since everyone knew?

No one wants to talk about it when it comes asking why anyone couldn't try to get custody of me when they first knew. Aunts and Cousins knew even kids I grew up with, and no one said or did anything. It's too late for what ifs and the why will never get answered, so I pray continually that I'm able to fully and wholeheartedly forgive everyone that knew and did nothing.

I will continue as long as I'm on this earth advocate for victims/survivors of domestic violence and child sexual abuse it was through writing this book that I can speak more about the sexual abuse side instead of just speaking about domestic violence. I know talking about child sexual abuse is uncomfortable, but it's happening to too many of our children. I encourage you to speak to your child and make them feel comfortable enough to come to you if something does happen and that you will support them no matter what.

Conclusion

The Secret that Everyone Knew was written to bring further awareness to domestic violence and child sexual abuse. Although I went through something that is considered hell, I want people to understand that it's okay to talk about it, especially, if you're someone who has survived.

If I could prevent one less day of domestic abuse, child sexual abuse or suicide among those who deal with this issue, this book has achieved its goal. If you are reading this book and are presently in a domestic violence situation, first and foremost your safety is important but here are a few things you can do.

1. Realize that even though he apologizes, he's going to hit you again.
2. Know that you are somebody to God.
3. Understand that there is a way out.
4. Seek help! DV professional, therapist, or someone you can trust that will help you to create a safe exit plan.
5. Keep all your essential documents in a safe place so when it's time to leave, the transition can be smooth.

If you are reading this book and starting a new relationship, here are a few things you should know about an abuser.

1. An abuser is always subtle at first with certain insults wrapped up in jokes.
2. He will romance you to no end.
3. He will want a commitment fast.
4. His red flags are there in front of you. If he starts secluding you from family and attempting to control your whereabouts, it will only escalate from there.
5. He is overly concerned.

If you are reading this book and you know someone in a domestic violence situation.

1. Pray for them daily.
2. Don't side with the abuser by giving them information on the one they're abusing.
3. Be a listening ear when needed.
4. Don't advise what they should do, especially, if you've never experienced abuse.
5. Help them with resources.

Here are a few resources you can share:

- National Domestic Violence Hotline 800-799-7233
- Stopitnow.org
- Crisitextline.org
- Rainn.org 800-656-HOPE
- National Suicide Prevention Lifeline 800-273-8255